Setting
Cambridge lies between the drained Fenland of Ely and the rolling Gog Magog hills to the south, but above all it is on a river. Almost the whole of the University was on one side of it until the 19th century. On the other are the Backs (of the colleges). The Cam was navigable from the sea only as far as here, and where one now strolls enjoying the river, there were once wharves for unloading the colleges' building materials. For Cambridge has no stone of its own but was supplied from quarries mainly in Northamptonshire, other materials used being clunch, a kind of stone-like chalk mined in the county, and brick.

Origins
The Romans had a town here of 25 acres on Castle Hill, overlooking the river crossing. The Normans placed a castle on this strategic point, after the Saxons had started the present town across the river. In the 13th century the annual Stourbridge Fair became a famous setting for trade. The town also had the income from a royal grant of a county-wide monopoly on unloading ships, and their tolls. But mediaeval Cambridge was a place of religious houses and churches increasingly interwoven with the University.

University
Some Oxford students _____ troubles at home _____ 1209. Still of mod_____ the University was _____ by the royal founda_____ Queens' Colleges i_____ and in 1496-1594 s_____ started. Colleges at _____ centres of teaching o_____ undergraduates lived _____ hostels until about 1500, some of which are commemorated in the names of buildings. The quantity of Victorian building at the old colleges and the creation of new ones accompanied a six-fold increase in student numbers during the 19th century, including girls from 1870. It also coincided with a great increase in the number of subjects taught, especially scientific ones after 1850.

Architecture
The colleges are very varied in their attractions, some displaying the magnificence of great benefactors, others revealing their impoverished mediaeval origins; so the grand may stand next to the intimate and the large jostle the small. Several are entered through splendid late mediaeval gatehouses with turrets and coats of arms. Wren was drawn to work here by an uncle, successively Master of Peterhouse and Bishop of Ely. After him came Haw_____ t, Cockerell _____ entury _____ ers of the _____ ld family. _____ many _____ k _____ tle _____ y in the _____, paving _____ cobbles of the courts, the fine doors to the gates, halls and chapels, and the Collyweston stone slates still on some roofs. One curiosity is the lanterns which sit astride many hall roofs; they recall the days when these rooms were heated by a fire on the floor and the smoke escaped through louvres. In Cambridge, closed-in college buildings and narrow lanes contrast with expansiveness and great vistas, and the informality of the streets with the orderliness of the University.

Modern Cambridge
May week, with its college balls and bumping races on the river, takes place in June, and there is honey for tea. King's has its Christmas carol service, and friends punt or stroll along the Backs. Cambridge is also a pleasant and airy centre of good shops, much of it pedestrianised, and of electronic industries further out.

Le Cadre

Cambridge est située entre la plaine marécageuse asséchée Fenland d'Ely et les collines vallonnées Gog Magog au sud, mais surtout, elle longe une rivière. Jusqu'au XIXe siècle, la plus grande partie de l'université se dressait d'un seul côté. De l'autre s'étendent les pelouses, appelées Backs, derrière les collèges. La Cam était navigable de la mer jusqu'à cette ville uniquement ; alors qu'aujourd'hui on se promène nonchalamment le long de la rivière, il y avait autrefois des quais pour décharger les matériaux de construction des collèges.

Les Origines

Les Romains avaient élevé une ville de quelque 10 hectares sur Castle Hill, dominant le passage de la rivière. Les Normands dressèrent un château en ce point stratégique, une fois que les Saxons eurent commencé d'établir la ville actuelle de l'autre côté de la rivière. Au XIIIe siècle, la foire annuelle de Stourbridge devint un lieu de rencontre célèbre pour le commerce. Mais la ville médiévale de Cambridge comprenait surtout des maisons religieuses et des églises qui tissèrent des liens de plus en plus étroits avec l'université.

L'Université

Des étudiants d'Oxford, fuyant des querelles intestines, vinrent s'installer ici en 1209. Encore d'envergure modeste en 1400, l'université s'agrandit considérablement avec les fondations royales des King's et Queens'Colleges en 1440 et 1448, par la suite sept autres collèges furent créés entre 1496 et 1594. Au début, les collèges étaient uniquement des centres d'enseignement, et les étudiants habitèrent dans des hostelleries jusqu'aux alentours de 1500, dont certaines sont commémorées dans les noms des établissements.

Le nombre des bâtiments victoriens dans les vieux collèges et la création de nouveaux établissements s'expliquent par le nombre des étudiants qui s'était multiplié par six au cours du XIXe siècle, les filles furent admises à partir de 1870.

L'Architecture

Les collèges sont de différents styles, certains affichent la splendeur de grands mécènes, d'autres révèlent leurs modestes origines médiévales ; le grandiose côtoie le modeste et l'imposant juxtapose le petit. Des loges splendides, style fin moyen-âge, avec tourelles et armoiries, ouvrent l'accès à certains collèges.

Wren fut appelé, pour travailler ici, par un oncle, successivement supérieur de Peterhouse et évêque d'Ely. Après lui vinrent Hawksmoor, Gibbs, Wyatt, Cockerell et Lutyens. Les bâtisseurs du XVIIe siècle furent souvent des membres de la famille Grumbold de réputation célèbre.

Les collèges ont aussi d'autres charmes, notamment les pelouses, les allées pavées des cours carrées, les portes élégantes des entrées, les halls et les chapelles, et les ardoises en pierre de Collyweston couvrant encore certains toits.

Cambridge Moderne

La semaine des courses à aviron, avec ses bals donnés dans les collèges et ses courses-poursuites sur la rivière, a lieu en juin ; il y a du miel au goûter.

Le King's a ses cantiques de Noël, et les étudiants se promènent en barques à fond plat gouvernées à la perche ou flânent sur les pelouses derrière les collèges. Cambridge est également une ville commerciale agréable avec de beaux magasins et de nombreuses rues piétonnières.

Lage

Cambridge liegt zwischen dem trockengelegten Moorland Fenland of Ely und den Gog Magog Hügeln im Süden, am Fluß Cam. Bis zum 19. Jahrhundert befand sich fast die ganze Universität auf einer Seite des Flusses. Auf der anderen Seite liegt der Park der Colleges "The Backs". Der Cam war vom Meer her nur bis hierher befahrbar. Wo man heute am Fluß entlang spazieren geht, standen früher Kais zum Entladen der Baustoffe für die Colleges.

Ursprünge

Die Römer hatten hier auf Castle Hill eine Stadt mit 10,1 ha Fläche, die den Flußübergang überblickte. Die Normannen erbauten an diesem strategischen Punkt eine Burg, nachdem die Angelsachsen die heutige Stadt auf der anderen Seite des Flusses begonnen hatten. Im 13. Jahrhundert wurde der Jahrmarkt Stourbridge Fair zu einem berühmten Knotenpunkt für den Handel. Das mittelalterliche Cambridge enthielt Ordenshäuser und Kirchen, deren Verknüpfung mit der Universität immer stärker zunahm.

Universität

Im Jahr 1209 ließen sich hier einige Oxford-Studenten nieder, die Problemen in ihrer Heimatuniversität entflohen waren. Die Universität, 1400 noch von bescheidener Größe, erhielt durch die königliche Gründung des King's und des Queens' Colleges in den Jahren 1440 und 1448 großen Auftrieb. In der Zeit von 1496 bis 1594 wurden noch sieben weitere Colleges begonnen. Colleges waren anfangs nur Bildungszentren, die Studenten wohnten bis etwa 1500 in Herbergen. An einige von ihnen erinnern noch Gebäudenamen.

Die viktorianischen Bauarbeiten an den alten Colleges und die Gründung neuer Colleges begleiteten während des 19. Jahrhunderts einen sechsfachen Anstieg der Zahl der Studenten, zu denen ab 1870 auch Studentinnen gehörten.

Architektur

Die Colleges haben sehr unterschiedliche Anziehungspunkte, einige zeigen die Großartigkeit bedeutender Gönner auf, andere lassen ihre verarmten mittelalterlichen Ursprünge erkennen. So kommt es, daß großartige Gebäude neben bescheidenen stehen und die großen sich mit den kleinen drängen. Mehrere Colleges haben als Eingang prachtvolle spätmittelalterliche Pförtnerhäuser mit Türmchen und Wappen.

Der berühmte britische Architekt Wren wurde von einem Onkel, der Rektor von Peterhouse und später Bischof von Ely war, zur Arbeit in Cambridge eingeladen. Nach ihm kamen Hawksmoor, Gibbs, Wyatt, Cockerell und Lutyens. Im 17. Jahrhundert waren die Baumeister oft Mitglieder der Grumbold-Familie.

In den Colleges findet der Besucher Rasenflächen, gepflasterte Höfe, prachtvolle Türen zu den Pförtnerhäusern, Aulen und Kapellen und die auf einigen Dächern noch vorhandenen Ziegel aus Collyweston-Stein.

Das Moderne Cambridge

May Week mit ihren College-Bällen und "Bumping"-Ruderregatta auf dem Fluß findet im Juni statt, und "... zum Tee gibt es Honig". King's College hält seinen berühmten Weihnachtslieder-Gottesdienst und man fährt mit Freunden im Stechkahn oder geht an den Backs entlang spazieren. Cambridge ist auch ein angenehmes und nonchalantes Zentrum guter Geschäfte, das weitgehend nur dem Fußgängerverkehr zugänglich ist.

Downing College

Downing should be approached from Regent Street. The only college founded between 1594 and 1869, it is appropriately different from all previous ones. It was begun in 1807, as a result of a bequest made by Sir George Downing in 1749 but contested by his family.

George III, when he heard of the proposal, only commented that he did not want it to be gothic; his wish was fulfilled, surprisingly, by the introduction of Greek architecture to Cambridge. William Wilkins (a Cambridge graduate) also designed a campus, the earliest of its kind in the world. But the litigation had reduced the endowment, and only part of his scheme was built. Downing has also led the way in reviving Classical architecture at Cambridge.

Emmanuel College

Emma now looks 18th-century from the street, but stands on the site of a Dominican Friary of which the church and a cloister range survived into the 18th century. Founded in 1584 as a Puritan college by Sir Walter Mildmay, Chancellor of the Exchequer, it has retained its early sympathies. John Harvard was a student here, emigrating in 1637, also John Cotton, Thomas Hooker and Samuel Stone, important men in the foundation of New England and Newtown College, which they renamed "Cambridge".

In 1930 some 17th-century bookcases from the old Library were given to Harvard College. The Chapel, directly opposite the front entrance, is a very early work by Wren. It is well worth seeing inside.

Christ's College

Lady Margaret Beaufort, Henry VII's mother, re-founded the college in 1505. It had originated in 1442 as a Grammar College called God's House, which was almost immediately moved here out of the way of the King's new College. The front gate (photo below) has fine original linenfold doors. Entrance Court is very largely 16th-century, although refaced in the 18th in Ketton stone, and its wistaria and magnolia add a softening touch. Milton studied at Christ's.

Downing College

On devrait aborder Downing par la Regent Street. Le seul collège à être fondé entre 1594 et 1869, il est à juste titre différent de tous les précédents. Sa construction commença en 1807 grâce au legs de Sir George Downing en 1749, qui fut contesté par sa famille.

En apprenant la proposition, George III déclara simplement qu'il ne voulait pas de style gothique ; son souhait fut exaucé, chose étonnante, par l'introduction de l'architecture grecque à Cambridge. Williams Wilkins (licencié de Cambridge) créa également un campus, le premier de son genre au monde.

Emmanuel College

Vues de la rue, les façades d'Emma appartiennent au XVIIIe siècle ; le collège est bâti sur le site d'une confrérie dominicaine dont l'église et un cloître ont survécu jusqu'au XVIIIe siècle. Collège puritain fondé en 1584, il a conservé ses premiers adeptes. John Harvard y fut étudiant avant d'émigrer en 1637, ainsi que John Cotton, Thomas Hooker et Samuel Stone, hommes importants dans la fondation de la Nouvelle-Angleterre et de Newton College qu'ils rebaptisèrent "Cambridge".

En 1930, quelques rayonnages datant du XVIIe siècle appartenant à l'ancienne bibliothèque furent donnés à Harvard College. La chapelle, située directement en face de l'entrée principale, est l'une des premières oeuvres de Wren. L'intérieur mérite une visite.

Christ's College

Lady Margaret Beaufort, la mère de Henry VII, fut la nouvelle fondatrice du collège en 1505. Ce dernier avait été créé à l'origine en 1442 en tant que lycée appelé God's House, qui fut presque immédiatement installé ici, à l'écart du nouveau King's College.

La cour d'entrée (photo à gauche) date essentiellement du XVIe siècle, malgré le nouveau revêtement en pierre de Ketton au XVIIIe siècle ; les glycines et les magnolias adoucissent les murs.

Downing College

Downing besucht man am besten von der Regent Street her. Dieses College war das einzige zwischen 1594 und 1869 gegründete und unterscheidet sich entsprechend stark von allen früheren Colleges. Mit seinem Bau wurde 1807 auf einen von Sir George Downing vermachten und von dessen Familie angefochtenen Nachlaß hin begonnen.

Als George III. von dem Vorschlag hörte, bemerkte er dazu nur, daß er es nicht wünschte, daß das College ein gothisches Gebäude würde. Sein Wunsch wurde erstaunlicherweise durch die Einführung griechischer Architektur in Cambridge erfüllt. William Wilkins (ein Cambridge-Graduierter) entwarf auch einen Campus, den frühesten seiner Art in der Welt.

Stained glass window at Emmanuel College, depicting John Harvard, Founder of Harvard University.

Emmanuel College

"Emma" sieht von der Straße gesehen wie ein Gebäude aus dem 18. Jahrhundert aus, es steht jedoch auf dem Gelände eines Dominikanerklosters, dessen Kirche und ein Kreuzgangbereich bis in das 18. Jahrhundert überlebten. Das College wurde 1584 als puritanisches College gegründet und hat seine anfänglichen Sympathien beibehalten. John Harvard war hier Student, (er emigrierte im Jahr 1637) ebenso John Cotton, Thomas Hooker und Samuel Stone, bedeutende Mitwirkende an der Gründung des New England and Newton College, das sie in "Cambridge" umbenannten.

1930 wurden dem Harvard College einige Bücherschränke aus dem 17. Jahrhundert aus der alten Bücherei übergeben. Die dem vorderen Eingang direkt gegenüberliegende Kapelle ist ein sehr frühes Werk von Wren. Ein Besuch dieser Kapelle lohnt sich sehr.

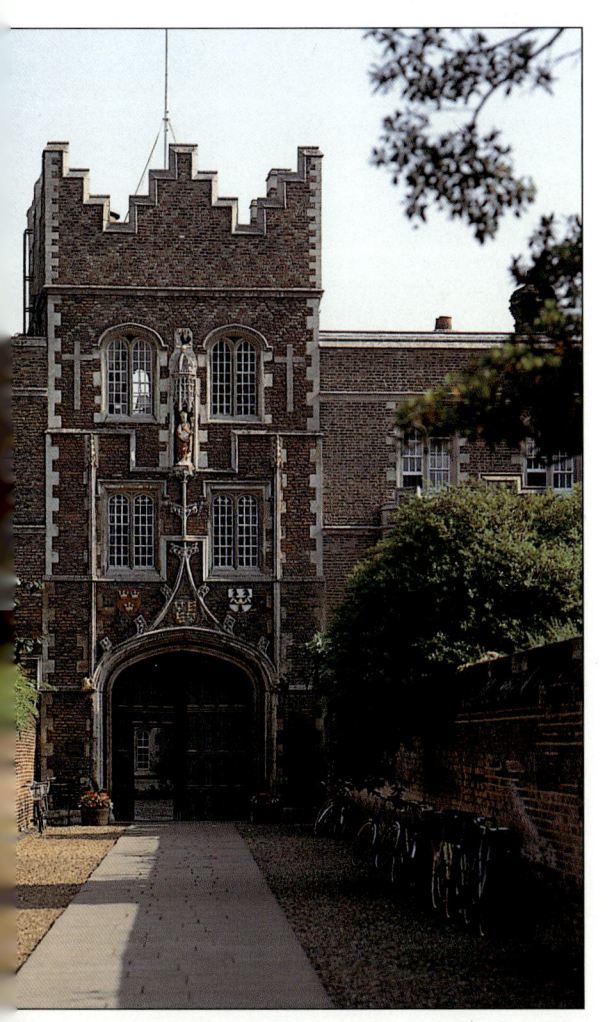

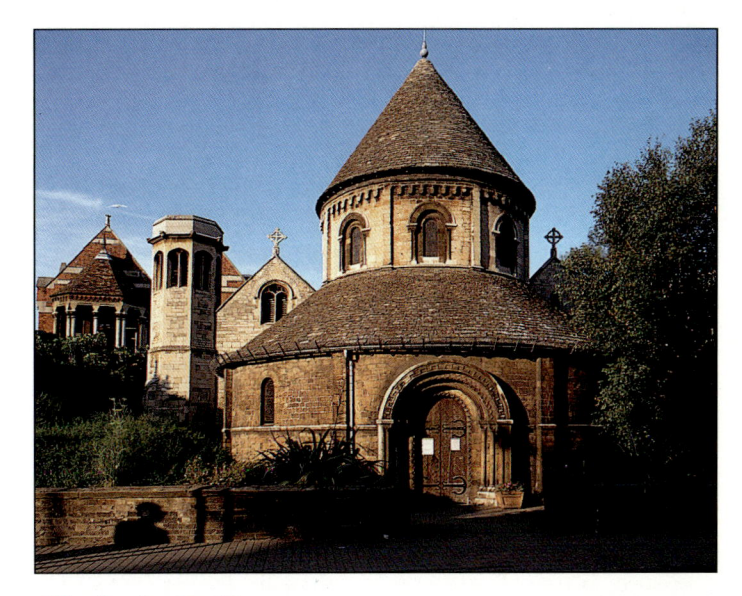

Christ's College

Lady Margaret Beaufort, die Mutter von Heinrich VII., gründete das College 1505 neu. Es war 1442 als ein God's House genanntes gymnasiales College entstanden, das fast sofort hierher verlegt wurde, um dem neuen College des Königs nicht im Weg zu sein.

Entrance Court (Foto Seite 4) ist weitgehend aus dem 16. Jahrhundert, obwohl es im 18. Jahrhundert eine neue Fassade aus Ketton-Stein erhielt, deren Strenge heute durch seine Glyzinien und Magnolie aufgelockert wird.

Sidney Sussex

Called after Lady Frances Sidney, whose will left (inadequate) money for its foundation, Sidney still has a close connection with her family, now Viscounts De L'Isle. It was built into the part-demolished ruins of the Franciscan Friary, bought from Trinity. The two old courts were modernised by Sir Jeffrey Wyatville in 1821 in Roman cement, which is now gradually being replaced with a stone facing.

Oliver Cromwell was at Sidney but the College supported the Crown in the Civil War. His portrait hangs by High Table and when the Fellows drink the Loyal Toast, his face is covered up by curtains.

The fine classical entrance gate of 1749 was moved to Jesus Lane by Wyatville, on your right on the way to:

Jesus College

Jesus (photo left) took over a mediaeval monastery, and is the only college to have substantial remains of one. Most of the 12th and 13th century church survives, the hall perpetuates the nuns' refectory and Cloister Court their cloisters, with a few monastic details uncovered here and there. The stone church with its tower, now the Chapel, is clearly visible on the right approaching the front gate. The college was founded by dissolving St Radegund's, which Bishop Alcock of Ely did in 1496. His new buildings are of diapered brick, and his cockerel rebus can be seen in several places. The range on the left of the gatehouse he built as a grammar school, but it was added to the college in 1570. The approach up the Chimney is through good early 18th-century gates.

The Round Church

There are only five circular Norman churches in England. Its shape results from the dedication, Holy Sepulchre, and the nave is surrounded by its aisle. In 1841 the church partly collapsed and the repair and restoration were undertaken in exemplary fashion (for the time) by the newly formed Cambridge Camden Society. The chancel was greatly enlarged in the 15th century and has carved angels in its roof. It is now a brass-rubbing centre.(photo above)

Bridge Street

Bridge Street (photo page 6) leads from the Round Church towards the Castle. On the right are two early 16th century houses, reminders that timber-framing was once more common in Cambridge; the two upper storeys project on timber jetties. St Clement's has a tower given in 1821 by a clergyman; because there was not room for it against the west end, it was built within the nave. Magdalene or Great Bridge crosses the Cam and is the successor to several earlier ones. On the right punts are for hire.

Magdalene College
Strong on lawyers and tradition, it was the last to take in girls (1988) and is the only college still to dine by candle-light alone (no slur on the food is implied). Magdalene has clearly seen a great change since 1546, when the newly founded college was reported to be extremely poor. In fact it has humble origins, as hostels started in 1428 for Benedictine monks studying law and theology. Parts of these buildings survive within later ones, and some peculiarities of the internal plan of First Court are caused by these 15th century origins.

Samuel Pepys, the diarist, bequeathed the college his library(photo right) and bookcases, in 1703, housed opposite the front entrance. Benson Court across the street was designed by Lutyens but only partly built. *Beyond the traffic lights, climb up to:*

Sidney Sussex
Tenant son nom de Lady Frances Sidney dont le testament procura les fonds (insuffisants) pour la fondation, Sidney entretient toujours des liens étroits avec sa famille, à présent Vicomtes De L'Isle. Le collège a été construit sur les vestiges d'un couvent franciscain acheté à Trinity.

Oliver Cromwell fit ses études à Sidney, mais le collège soutint la Couronne pendant la guerre civile. Son portrait est accroché au-dessus de la table des professeurs, au réfectoire, et lorsque ces derniers portent un toast à la reine, son visage est caché par des rideaux.

L'élégante porte d'entrée classique de 1749 fut déplacée dans *Jesus Lane par Wyatville, à droite, en route vers:*

Jesus College
Jesus, (photo page 4-5) installé dans un couvent médiéval, est le seul collège à avoir gardé des vestiges importants. La plus grande partie de l'église du XIIe et XIIIe siècle subsiste, le hall perpétue le réfectoire des religieuses et la Cloister Court leur cloître, avec quelques détails monastiques découverts ici et là. L'église en pierre avec son clocher, à présent la Chapelle, est nettement visible sur la droite en approchant de la porte principale ; elle comporte de belles boiseries par Pugin, les vitraux sont réalisés par Burne Jones et des plafonds par William Morris.(photo...)

Round Church - L'Eglise Ronde
Il n'y a que cinq églises rondes d'architecture romane en Angleterre. La forme de l'église est due à sa consécration, le Saint Sépulcre, et la nef est entourée de ses bas-côtés. Le choeur a été considérablement élargi au XVe siècle et des anges ont été sculptés dans son plafond. C'est à présent un centre de décalque et de frottement de plaques en cuivre. (photo page 5)

Bridge Street
Bridge Street(photo à gauche) conduit de l'église Round Church au château. A droite se dressent deux maisons du début du XVIe siècle, souvenirs d'une époque où les charpentes en bois étaient courantes à Cambridge ; les deux étages supérieurs s'avancent sur des jetées en bois. St Clement's comporte une tour donnée par un ecclésiastique en 1821 ; parce qu'il n'y avait pas suffisamment de place contre le côté ouest, elle fut construite dans la nef. Le pont Magdalene ou Great Bridge traverse la Cam, c'est le successeur de plusieurs autres auparavant. A droite, on peut louer des bateaux plats que l'on gouverne à la perche.

Magdalene College
Fortement attaché à la tradition et spécialisé dans les études de droit, le collège fut le dernier à admettre des filles (1988).
Magdalene a manifestement subi un grand changement depuis 1546, lorsque le collège récemment fondé fut déclaré être extrêmement pauvre. En effet, il a connu d'humbles origines, lorsque des foyers commencèrent de s'ouvrir en 1428 pour les moines bénédictins étudiant le droit et la théologie. Une partie de ces bâtiments subsiste dans ceux de temps plus récents, et certaines particularités du plan intérieur de la

première cour témoignent des origines du XVe siècle.

En 1703, le chroniqueur Samuel Pepys légua au collège sa bibliothèque(photo ci-dessous) et ses casiers de rangement qui sont abrités en face de l'entrée centrale. *Après les feux, grimpez jusqu'à:*

Sidney Sussex College

Sidney wurde nach Lady Frances Sidney benannt, die in ihrem Testament (nicht ausreichende) Mittel für seine Gründung hinterließ. Es hat immer noch eine enge Verbindung mit der Familie, den heutigen Viscounts De L'Isle. Es wurde in die teilweise abgerissenen Ruinen des Franziskanerklosters hineingebaut, die Trinity abgekauft wurden.

Oliver Cromwell war in Sidney, das College war aber im englischen Bürgerkrieg auf der Seite der Krone. Cromwells Porträt hängt beim "High Table", und wenn die "Fellows" den "Loyal Toast" trinken, wird sein Gesicht mit Vorhängen verdeckt.

Das schöne klassische Eingangstor von 1749 wurde von Wyatville in die Jesus Lane verlegt, rechts auf Ihrem Weg zum:

Jesus College

Jesus College (Foto Seite 4-5) übernahm ein mittelalterliches Kloster und ist das einzige College, das noch beträchtliche Reste eines solchen aufweist. Die Kirche aus dem 12. und 13. Jahrhundert ist noch weitgehend vorhanden, die "Hall" ist das renovierte Refektorium der Nonnen und Cloister Court ihre Kreuzgänge, in denen hier und da noch einige klösterliche Details freigelegt sind.

Round Church

In Englang gibt es nur fünf runde normannische Kirchen, zu denen auch "The Round Church" gehört. Ihre Form geht auf das Heilige Grab zurück, ihr Hauptschiff ist von ihrem Mittelschiff umgeben. Der Chor wurde im 15. Jahrhundert stark vergrößert und hat auf seinem Dach geschnitzte Engelfiguren. Heute ist es ein Zentrum für das "Brass-Rubbing"-Hobby, dem Durchpausen der Bilder auf Messinggrabtafeln. (Foto Seite 5)

Bridge Street

Bridge Street (Foto Seite 6) führt von der Round Church zur Burg. Auf ihrer rechten Seite liegen zwei Häuser aus dem frühen 16. Jahrhundert, die daran erinnern, daß es in Cambridge früher viel mehr Fachwerkhäuser gab. Die beiden Obergeschosse sind auf Holzträgern vorstehend aufgesetzt. St Clement's erhielt 1821 von einem Geistlichen einen Turm; am Westende der Kirche war jedoch kein Platz für ihn, weshalb er im Hauptschiff gebaut wurde.

Die Brücke Magdalene oder Great Bridge überspannt den Cam und ist Nachfolger mehrerer früherer Brücken. Rechts sind Stechkähne zu mieten.

Magdalene College

Dieses an Juristen und Traditionen reiche College nahm als letztes der Colleges Studentinnen auf (1988). Magdalene hat sich seit 1546, als das gerade neugegründete College als extrem arm gemeldet wurde, eindeutig stark verändert. Seine Ursprünge sind bescheiden: sie gehen auf 1428 begonnene Herbergen für Jura und Theologie studierende Benediktiner-Mönche zurück. Teile dieser Gebäude bestehen noch innerhalb späterer Gebäude, und einige der Eigenheiten des Innenplanes des First Courts sind durch diese Ursprünge im 15. Jahrhundert begründet.

Der Chronist Samuel Pepys vermachte dem College 1703 seine Bibliothek (Foto links) und Bücherschränke, die nun gegenüber dem vorderen College-Eingang ihre Heimat haben. *Begeben Sie sich auf der anderen Seite der Kreuzung zum:*

Castle Hill
The Castle is now only a steep mound behind the Castle pub (photo right). For two centuries it functioned as a royal castle and gaol, built by William the Conqueror in 1068. Its buildings have gone, demolished to build King's, Emmanuel, Magdalene and Great St Mary's, until in 1606 only a gatehouse used as a prison and some ruins remained.

Kettle's Yard Art Gallery
This is 'something completely different'. Here is a collection of 20th-century paintings and sculptures by world-famous artists. They represent the taste of one man, Jim Ede, some-time curator of the Tate Gallery. There are also changing exhibitions and a good art bookshop. Relax and be exhilarated.

St John's
Definitely one of the largest colleges, (photos pages 8-10) it has a chapel as big as Oxford Cathedral. There is a vista straight through the first three courts, which (excepting Scott's high Victorian chapel) were built between 1510 and 1671. The front gatehouse set in its flanking ranges is perhaps the loveliest in Cambridge, of early Tudor brickwork; that between the next two courts is called the Shrewsbury Tower after a Countess who helped to pay for Second Court in about 1600. The College is named after the Hospital of St John, which survived until 1869. New Court stands on the Backs: a scheme to landscape them as a whole, conceived in 1779 by Capability Brown, had been shelved and was therefore not interrupted by it. Built in 1826-31, it is crowned by the Wedding Cake, a cupola lighting the staircase. Reach it by the Bridge of Sighs (photo page 10), and admire the view of it up the Backs.

The School Of Pythagoras
At the back of St John's, the 'School' dates from about 1200. It was built of stone and clunch as a house; as such it is much the earliest in Cambridge and one of the oldest in England. The back range was added in the 16th and 17th centuries. The name dates from the 16th century and seems to be entirely whimsical.

Castle Hill

Le château n'est plus maintenant qu'une butte escarpée derrière le Castle pub(photo à gauche). Construit en 1068 par Guillaume le Conquérant, il a servi de château royal et de prison pendant deux siècles. Ses bâtiments ont disparu, démolis pour construire King's, Emmanuel, Magdalene et Great St Mary's, jusqu'à ce qu'il ne reste plus en 1606 qu'une loge servant de prison et quelques ruines.

La Galerie D'Art Kettle's Yard

Voici "quelque chose de totalement différent". Il s'agit d'une collection de peintures et de sculptures du XXe siècle réalisées par des artistes célèbres dans le monde entier. Il y a également des expositions organisées régulièrement, ainsi qu'une librairie de livres d'art bien achalandée. Détendez-vous dans l'allégresse.

St John's

Assurément l'un des plus grands collèges, (photo pages 8-10) avec une chapelle aussi grande que la cathédrale d'Oxford. Une vue directe plonge sur les trois premières cours qui (à l'exception de la haute chapelle victorienne de Scott) furent construites entre 1510 et 1671. Dans le prolongement, la loge principale en brique, début style Tudor, est peut-être la plus jolie de Cambridge ; entre les deux cours suivantes s'élève la Tour Shrewsbury qui doit son nom à une comtesse ayant contribué au financement de la seconde cour vers 1600. La nouvelle cour s'étend sur les Backs. Construite en 1826-31, elle est couronnée par le Wedding Cake (Gâteau de noce), un dôme éclairant l'escalier. Vous pouvez l'atteindre par le Bridge of Sighs (le Pont des Soupirs) et en admirer la vue en remontant les Backs. (photo page 10)

L'Ecole De Pythagore

Située à l'arrière de St John's, "l'Ecole" date de 1200 environ. Elle est construite en pierre et en argile schisteuse comme une maison ; à ce point de vue, elle est sans doute la première de son genre à Cambridge et l'une des plus anciennes en Angleterre.

Son nom date du XVIe siècle et semble tout à fait fantaisiste.

Castle Hill

Die Burg ist heute nur noch ein steiler Hügel hinter dem Castle Pub. (Foto links) Die im Jahr 1068 von Wilhelm dem Eroberer erbaute Burg diente zwei Jahrhunderte lang als königliche Burg und Gefängnis. Ihre Gebäude wurden zum Bau von King´s, Emmanuel, Magdalene und Great St Mary´s abgerissen, bis im Jahr 1606 nur noch ein als Gefängnis benutztes Pförtnerhaus und einige Ruinen übrig waren.

Kettle's Yard Art Gallery

Diese Kunstgalerie ist "etwas ganz anderes": Sie enthält eine Sammlung von Gemälden und Skulpturen weltberühmter Künstler des 20. Jahrhunderts, Wanderausstellungen und eine gute Kunstbuchhandlung. Hier können Sie sich entspannen und anregen lassen.

St John's

St John's (Foto Seites 8-10) ist eindeutig eines der größten Colleges und hat eine Kapelle, die so groß ist wie die Kathedrale in Oxford. Hier bietet sich ein Blick durch die ersten drei Höfe hindurch, die (mit Ausnahme von Scotts hoher viktorianischer Kapelle) zwischen 1510 und 1671 gebaut wurden. Das vordere Pförtnerhaus ist mit seinem Mauerwerk aus der frühen Tudorzeit vielleicht das hübscheste in ganz Cambridge. Das Pförtnerhaus zwischen den nächsten beiden Höfen wird nach einer Gräfin, die etwa 1600 den Bau des Second Courts (d.h. des zweiten Courts) finanziell mitunterstützte, Shrewsbury Tower genannt.

New Court steht auf den Backs. Es wurde 1826 bis 1831 erbaut und mit der "Wedding Cake" (Hochzeitstorte) genannten Kuppel gekrönt, durch die Licht auf die Treppe einfällt. Überqueren Sie die "Bridge of Sighs" (Foto oben) zum New Court und bewundern Sie die Aussicht auf die Backs von hier.

The School Of Pythagoras

Die "Schule des Pythagoras" liegt an der Rückseite von St John's. Sie wurde etwa 1200 als Haus aus Stein und Pfeifenton gebaut und ist das früheste seiner Art in Cambridge und eines der ältesten in England.

Der Name stammt aus dem 16. Jahrhundert und scheint einfach auf einer schnurrigen Idee zu beruhen.

Trinity College

Trinity (photos page 11 and 12) is understandably the one chosen by members of the Royal Family staying in Cambridge. There are two main courts. Great Court dates from about 1600, when the existing college was enlarged to form this most spacious of all courts. The other is Nevile's Court, which is only slightly later, and both are essentially the inspiration (and in part the gift) of 'the splendid, courteous and bountiful' Dr Thomas Nevile, Master 1593-1615.

Nevile's Fountain in the middle of Great Court is one of the finest examples of Elizabethan design in Cambridge; it was originally painted and gilded and is still fed by a duct dating from 1327. The Hall, built in 1605 after careful consideration of the best halls in London, especially Middle Temple's, is also exceptional with a marvellous interior. Wren's Library (photo below , library bottom left), closing Nevile's Court from the river, is simply one of the most perfect rooms of its period in England. He gave his work without fee, and it remains complete with its bookcases and tables, the carving by Grinling Gibbons.

Detail of Trinity College's Great Gate.

Gonville And Caius

The name derives from Gonville Hall, called after its founder of 1348, and Dr Caius, Master 1559-73. The college is always called Caius (pronounced 'keys'). Gonville Court, although later refaced and heavily treated by the architect Waterhouse in 1870, remains its 14th-century size.

Dr Caius added Caius Court, making it only the second college to have two courts. He deliberately left one side open to encourage the circulation of air, an idea copied at other Cambridge colleges, such as both the old courts at Sidney Sussex. Padua-trained, he had become personal physician to Edward VI and Mary, and knew something of Italian architecture. His Gates of Virtue and Honour(photo page 12) are two of the first serious attempts in England to build in the classical style.

The college unfortunately provides an irresistible temptation to the Cambridge Climbers to try the Senate House leap-to jump across Senate House Passage from the College roof.

Trinty Hall

This college(photo page 13) was established in 1350 by Bishop Bateman of Norwich for 'scholars of the Holy Trinity of Norwich'. It was founded for a specific purpose, the study of Canon and Civil Law, and remains strongly associated with legal training. No doubt it was the bishop's idea to include a chapel in the plan, previous colleges having made use of the nearest church. Trinity Hall also has a long tradition of rowing, and the only independently endowed boat club. Front Court is largely 14th century, although cloaked in an urbane frontage of Ketton stone in 1743.

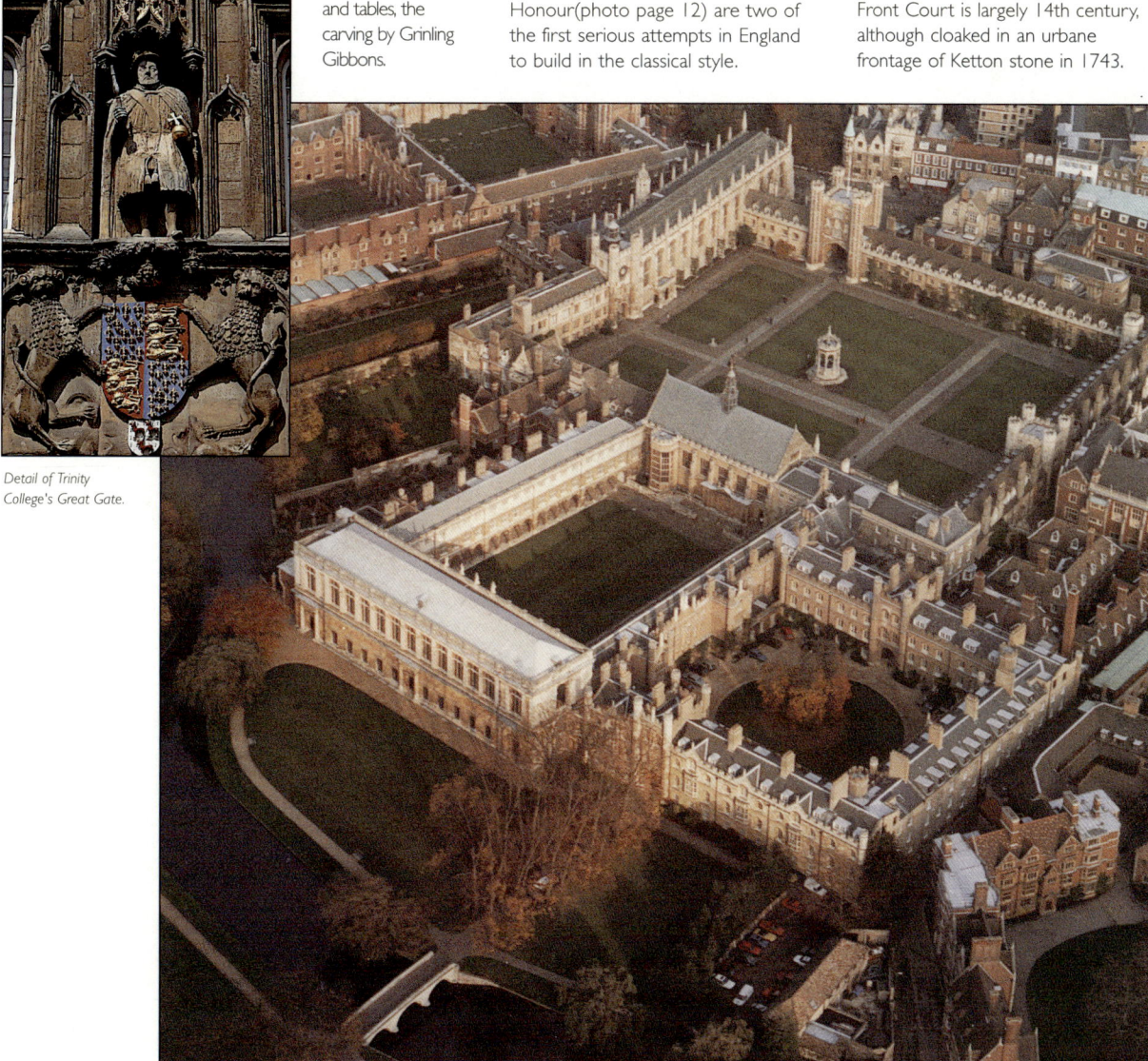

11

Above: Trinity Street

Trinity College

Trinity (photo page 11 et ci-dessus) est naturellement le collège choisi par les membres de la famille royale étudiant à Cambridge. Il compte deux cours d'honneur. Great Court date de 1600 environ, lorsque le collège d'alors fut agrandi pour former cette cour des plus spacieuses. L'autre, Nevile's Court, fut construite légèrement plus tard. Toutes les deux furent essentiellement le résultat de l'inspiration (et en partie du don) du "splendide, courtois et généreux" Dr Thomas Nevile, supérieur du collège de 1593 à 1615.

La fontaine de Nevile qui se dresse au milieu de Great Court, est l'un des plus magnifiques exemples du style élisabéthain à Cambridge ; à l'origine, peinte et dorée, elle est toujours alimentée par une canalisation qui remonte à 1327. Le Hall, construit en 1605 après avoir soigneusement étudié les plus beaux Halls de Londres, particulièrement celui de Middle Temple's, est également exceptionnel avec son superbe décor intérieur. La bibliothèque de Wren, (photo...) qui referme la Nevile's Court du côté de la rivière, est tout simplement l'une des salles les plus parfaites de cette époque en Angleterre.

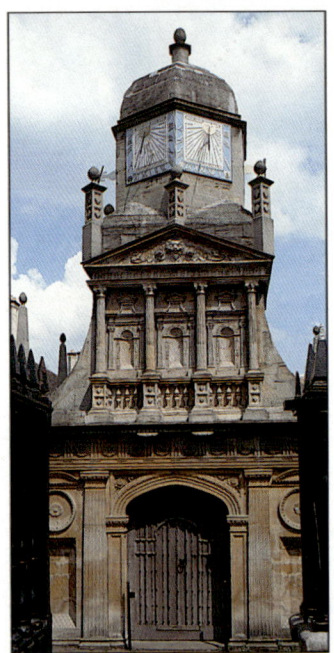

Gates of Honour, Gonville & Caius

Gonville Et Caius

Son nom provient de Gonville Hall, ainsi nommé d'après son fondateur en 1348, et d'après le Dr Caius. Bien que la façade et l'aspect de la Gonvile Court aient été fortement modifiés par l'architecte Waterhouse en 1870, elle conserve ses dimensions du XIVe siècle.

Le Dr Caius ajouta la Caius Court, ce qui en fit le deuxième collège seulement à bénéficier d'une seconde cour.

Le collège offre malheureusement la tentation irrésistible aux grimpeurs de Cambridge de faire le saut de la Senate House, c'est-à-dire d'enjamber l'allée de la Senate House à partir du toit du collège.

Trinity Hall

Ce collège (photo page 13) a été établi en 1350 par Bateman, evêque de Norwich, pour les "étudiants de Holy Trinity de Norwich". Fondé dans un but particulier, à savoir l'étude du droit canon et du droit romain, il reste fortement associé à la formation juridique. Il ne fait pas de doute que l'évêque avait l'intention d'inclure une chapelle dans ses plans, car les collèges précédents avaient accaparé l'église la plus proche. La Front Court date principalement du XIVe siècle, bien qu'elle ait été revêtue en 1743 d'une façade urbaine en pierre de Ketton.

Trinity Hall Library

Trinity College

Trinity (Foto Seite 11 and 12) ist verständlicherweise das von in Cambridge weilenden Mitgliedern des britischen Königshauses gewählte. Es hat zwei Haupthöfe: Great Court stammt aus etwa 1600, als das bestehende College vergrößert wurde, um diesen geräumigsten aller Höfe zu formen. Der andere ist Nevile's Court, der nur geringfügig jünger ist. Beide Courts sind im wesentlichen die Inspiration (und teilweise auch das Geschenk) des "großartigen, höflichen und großzügigen" Dr. Thomas Nevile, Rektor von 1593 - 1615.

Der Brunnen Nevile's Fountain in der Mitte des Great Courts ist eines der besten Beispiele eines elisabethanischen Entwurfs in Cambridge, usprünglich war er bemalt und vergoldet. Seine Wasserleitung stammt noch aus dem Jahr 1327. Die College-Hall wurde 1605 nach sorgfältiger Erörterung der besten derartigen Gebäude in London, besonders das des Middle Temples in London, gebaut und ist auch in seinem Inneren besonders prachtvoll. Wren´s Library, die(Foto...) Nevile's Court vom Fluß her abschließt, ist einfach einer der perfektesten Räume seiner Zeit in England.

Gonville und Caius College

Der Name stammt von Gonville Hall, die 1348 nach ihrem Gründer benannt wurde, und Dr. Caius, Rektor von 1559 - 1573. Das College wird immer nur Caius (wird "kies" betont). Gonville Court ist zwar noch so groß wie im 14. Jahrhundert, erhielt aber später eine neue Fassade und wurde 1870 vom Architekten Waterhouse stark geändert.

Dr Caius fügte Caius Court hinzu, wodurch es zum zweiten von nur zwei Colleges mit zwei Courts wurde.

Unglücklicherweise lockt das College die Cambridge Climbers mit der unwiderstehlichen Herausforderung, den "Senator House Sprung" zu wagen, d.h. vom College-Dach über die Senate House Passage zu springen.

Trinity Hall

Dieses College wurde (Foto oben) 1350 von Bishof Bateman von Norwich für "Studenten der Heiligen Dreifaltigkeit in Norwich" gegründet. Es wurde für einen bestimmten Zweck gegründet, das Studium von kanonischem und bürgerlichem Recht, und ist auch heute noch stark mit juristischer Ausbildung assoziiert. Zweifellos war es die Idee des Bischofs, eine Kapelle in seinen Plan aufzunehmen. Bis dahin hatten Colleges immer die ihnen am nächsten gelegene Kirche benutzt.

Front Court ist weitgehend aus dem 14. Jahrhundert, es erhielt jedoch 1743 eine städtische Fassade aus Ketton-Stein.

Clare College

Clare(photo below page 14-15) is the second oldest surviving college, having been started in 1326 as University Hall. However, the buildings were systematically replaced, mostly in 1638-1693, to a harmonious design. Four of the Grumbolds worked here as masons and they gave the front gateway a fan vault in 1640. There is a view from Trinity Lane straight through forecourt, college and gardens, and across the river. The bridge(photo right) is the first classical one at Cambridge and perhaps the most delightful. It dates from 1638 and the panels are carved with various nautical allusions. The gates here are some of the earliest and loveliest wrought ironwork in Cambridge.

The Old Schools

The outer court was the old King's College; the inner court straight ahead houses the original University buildings. The old court of King's was only sold to the University in 1829. All that remains of the College is the gatehouse(photo right), its foundation-stone laid by Henry VI in 1441, but left unfinished until 1890. The inner court remains 14th and 15th century on three sides; here were the University's first buildings designed for teaching Divinity and Canon and Civil Law, together with their libraries. The east side was handsomely rebuilt in 1754. It was intended to be part of an open three sided court with:

The Senate House

The problems of housing the University and its libraries plagued the 18th century. Frustrated proposals to rebuild the Old Schools were drawn up by Wren, Hawksmoor, Gibbs, Adam, Soane and others, resulting in individual buildings by different architects. The earliest was the Senate House, (photo above) built in 1722 by James Gibbs; it is one of Cambridge's most distinguished buildings and marvellously sited, terminating the view up King's Parade. It was built on the site of some houses, following a substantial gift of books by George I. The books were housed elsewhere and it was designed as a room for University meetings. Within are statues by Nollekens and Rysbrack and the unusually massive railings outside are original.

Great St Mary's

The University Church(photo page 15) has a particularly fine interior. It was mostly rebuilt in 1473-1514, with the help of many wealthy patrons, but the tower was only finished in 1608. Until the Senate House was commissioned, University ceremonies such as the conferring of degrees, and disputations, were held here. Inevitably it was the centre of the controversy which absorbed the University at the Reformation, with sermons preached by Latimer and the great names of the day. Among its intriguing features are the two organs, one belonging to the University and one to the parish, and an oak pulpit which can be slid on rails into the middle of the church for University sermons. The clock(photo below) was given chimes in 1793, thought to have been composed by two undergraduates, and subsequently made famous by Big Ben as 'Westminster chimes'.

Clare College
Clare College (photo page 14-15) est le deuxième collège le plus ancien ayant survécu de cette époque, ayant débuté en 1326 sous le nom de University Hall. Toutefois, les bâtiments ont fait l'objet d'un remplacement systématique, principalement de 1638 à 1693, pour adopter une architecture harmonieuse.

La vue s'ouvre directement de Trinity Lane sur la première cour, le collège et les jardins, puis de l'autre côté de la rivière.

Le pont (photo à gauche) est le premier pont de style classique de Cambridge, et peut-être le plus agréable. Il remonte à 1638, et est orné de panneaux sculptés représentant diverses scènes aux allusions nautiques.

Les Old Schools
La cour extérieure était l'ancien King's College ; la cour intérieure, tout droit devant celle-ci, abrite les bâtiments de l'université originale. Il ne reste plus du College que sa loge.

La cour intérieure conserve ses vestiges du XIVe et du XVe siècle sur trois côtés ; c'étaient les premières salles de l'université conçues pour l'enseignement de la théologie, ainsi que du droit canon et du droit romain, flanquées de leurs bibliothèques. La façade à l'est fut magnifiquement refaite en 1754. Elle devait faire partie d'une court à trois côtés avec :

La Senate House
Tout au long du XVIIIe siècle, il y eut des problèmes pour loger l'université et ses bibliothèques. Wren, Hawksmoor, Gibbs, Adam, Soane et d'autres firent en vain des propositions pour reconstruire les Old Schools, ce qui aboutit à une juxtaposition de bâtiments individuels par différents architectes.

Le plus ancien fut la Senate (photo page 14) House, construite en 1722 par James Gibbs ; c'est l'un des bâtiments les plus raffinés de Cambridge, dans un emplacement merveilleux, mettant un point final à la vue remontant King's Parade. Elle fut érigée sur le site de plusieurs demeures, à la suite d'une donation importante de livres par George Ier. Ces livres furent abrités ailleurs, et elle fut conçue comme salle de réunions pour l'université.

St Mary's The Great
L'église de l'université (photo ci-dessous) se remarque par son intérieur magnifique. Jusqu'à l'établissement de la Senate House, c'est là que se déroulaient les cérémonies universitaires, notamment la remise des diplômes. Parmi ses atours fascinants se trouvent deux orgues, l'un appartenant à l'université et l'autre à la paroisse, ainsi qu'une chaire en chêne qui, pour les sermons universitaires, peut se déplacer sur des glissières jusqu'au milieu de l'église. L'horloge(photo à gauche) reçut un carillon en 1793, que l'on croit avoir été composé par deux étudiants, et qui fut rendu célèbre par la suite par Big Ben sous le nom de "carillon de Westminster".

Clare College

Clare (Foto Seite 14-15) ist das zweitälteste noch vorhandene College und war 1326 als University Hall begonnen worden. Die Gebäude wurde jedoch systematisch durch neue, miteinander harmonisierende ersetzt, hauptsächlich in der Zeit von 1638 bis 1693.

Man kann von Trinity Lane direkt durch Vorhof, College und Park bis über den Fluß blicken.

Die Brücke (Foto Seite 14) ist die erste klassische in Cambridge und vielleicht auch die hübscheste. Sie stammt aus dem Jahr 1638. In ihre Seitenplatten sind verschiedene nautische Anspielungen eingehauen.

The Old Schools

Der äußere Court war das alte King's College, der innere (geradeaus) enthält die ursprünglichen Universitätsgebäude. Vom College ist nur noch das Pförtnerhaus vorhanden. Die Gebäude des inneren Courts sind an drei Seiten noch aus dem 14. und 15. Jahrhundert: Hier befanden sich die ersten Gebäude der Universität für das Studium von Theologie und kanonischem und bürgerlichem Recht zusammen mit ihren Bibliotheken. Die Ostseite wurde 1754 neu aufgebaut. Sie sollte Teil eines offenen, dreiseitigen Courts mit den folgenden Gebäuden sein:

Senate House

Im 18. Jahrhundert gab es viele Probleme mit der Unterbringung der Universität und ihrer Bibliotheken. Zu den frustrierten Vorschlägen für den Wiederaufbau der Old Schools gehörten Entwürfe von Wren, Hawksmoor, Gibbs, Adam, Soane und anderen, was einzelne Gebäude von verschiedenen Architekten zur Folge hatte.

Das älteste dieser Gebäude war Senate House, (Foto Seite 14) das 1722 von James Gibbs erbaut wurde. Es ist eines der distinguiertesten Gebäude von Cambridge und mit seiner Lage am Ende der Aussicht auf die King's Parade hervorragend positioniert. Es wurde auf ein umfangreiches Büchergeschenk von George I. hin erbaut. Die Bücher wurden jedoch in einem anderen Gebäude untergebracht und Senate House wurde als Raum für Universitätssitzungen bestimmt.

Great St Mary's

Das Innere der Universitätskirche ist besonders schön. Der Neuaufbau der Kirche fand mit Hilfe vieler wohlhabender Gönner hauptsächlich von 1473 bis 1514 statt, der Turm wurde jedoch erst 1608 fertiggestellt. Bis zur Fertigstellung des Senate House fanden Universitätszeremonien, wie Gradverleihung und Dispute, hier statt.

Zu ihren interessantesten Merkmalen gehören die zwei Orgeln, von denen eine der Universität und die andere der Pfarrei gehört, und eine Eichenkanzel, die für Universitätspredigten auf Schienen in die Mitte der Kirche geschoben werden kann. Die Uhr erhielt ihr Glockenspiel im Jahr 1793, das angeblich von zwei Studenten komponiert worden war und später durch Big Ben als "Westminster Chimes" berühmt wurde. (Foto Seite 15)

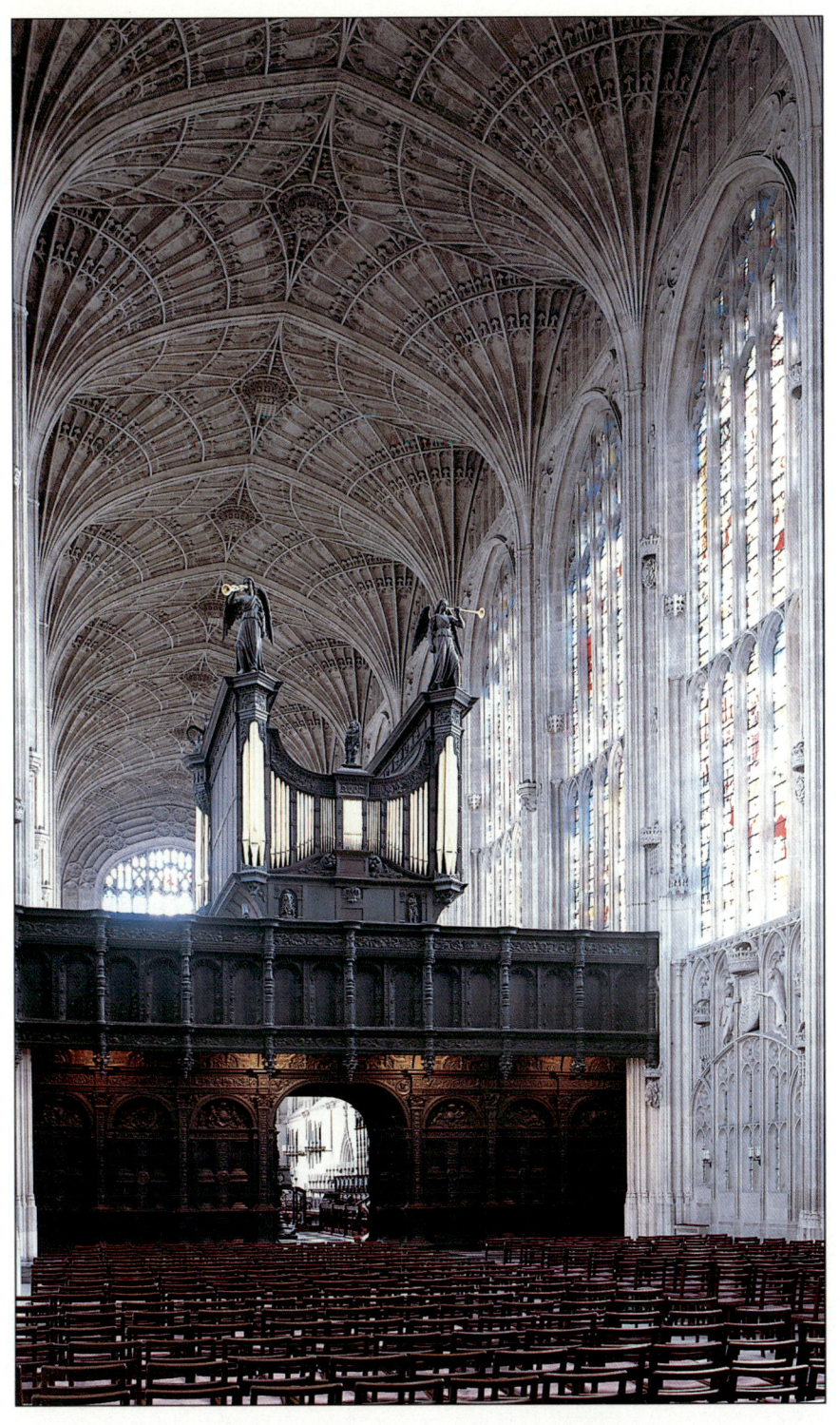

King's College

King's (photos pages 16-18) was founded on a bold scale, befitting a king. Several streets had to be suppressed and a church and at least one other college cleared from the site. But it took a long time to build. The College is unusually simple architecturally, Great Court being of only three periods. The Chapel(photo above) was begun in 1446 by Henry VI and continued through five reigns until ready for use in 1538; only royal finance could have seen it through. William Camden commented in 1586 that the 'Chapel may rightly be counted one of the fairest buildings of the whole world'. The fan vaulting, stained glass, and the wooden screen with its heraldic devices of Henry VIII and Anne Boleyn, are early 16th century and supreme of their kind. The Gibbs Building dates from 1723 and is named after its architect. It houses the Fellows and was the only result, in the 18th century, of plans for completing the college drawn up by Hawksmoor and Wren, Gibbs, Adam and Wyatt, but abandoned for lack of money.

Queens' College

The college(photo page 19) is down Queens' Lane, which joined onto Trinity Lane until King's was built. It takes its name from Margaret of Anjou, queen to Henry VI, who established it in 1448, and Elizabeth Woodville, queen to Edward IV, who endowed it. Front Court is the University's first brick court and survives complete enough to give a very good idea of its original appearance. The painted dial(photo page 19) is thought to originate in the mid-17th century; it has sun and moon dials and the signs of the zodiac. Cloister Court is also mainly 15th century and a delightful place to walk with its brick arcades. The President's Lodge on the right is a little later and is unique among the colleges for its handsome timber-framing, with bay and oriel windows. The legend that the wooden bridge(photo page 20) over the Cam was designed by a 17th-century mathematician and built without fastenings remains - a legend. It dates from 1749 and was the work of an inventive master-carpenter called Etheridge; it was renewed in 1902. Hire another punt in the Mill Pool just below the bridge.

St Catherine's

Cat's was founded in 1475 by Robert Woodlark, Provost of King's, and one of the duties of its Fellows was to pray for the souls of their benefactors. It was completely rebuilt and enlarged in the 17th and 18th centuries. Until the 18th century Cat's was entered from the rear, through the gateway onto Queens' Lane, but the purchase and demolition of houses enabled the frontage with its railings to be opened up. The windows in part of the right-hand range were altered to the Tudor-gothic style in 1868.

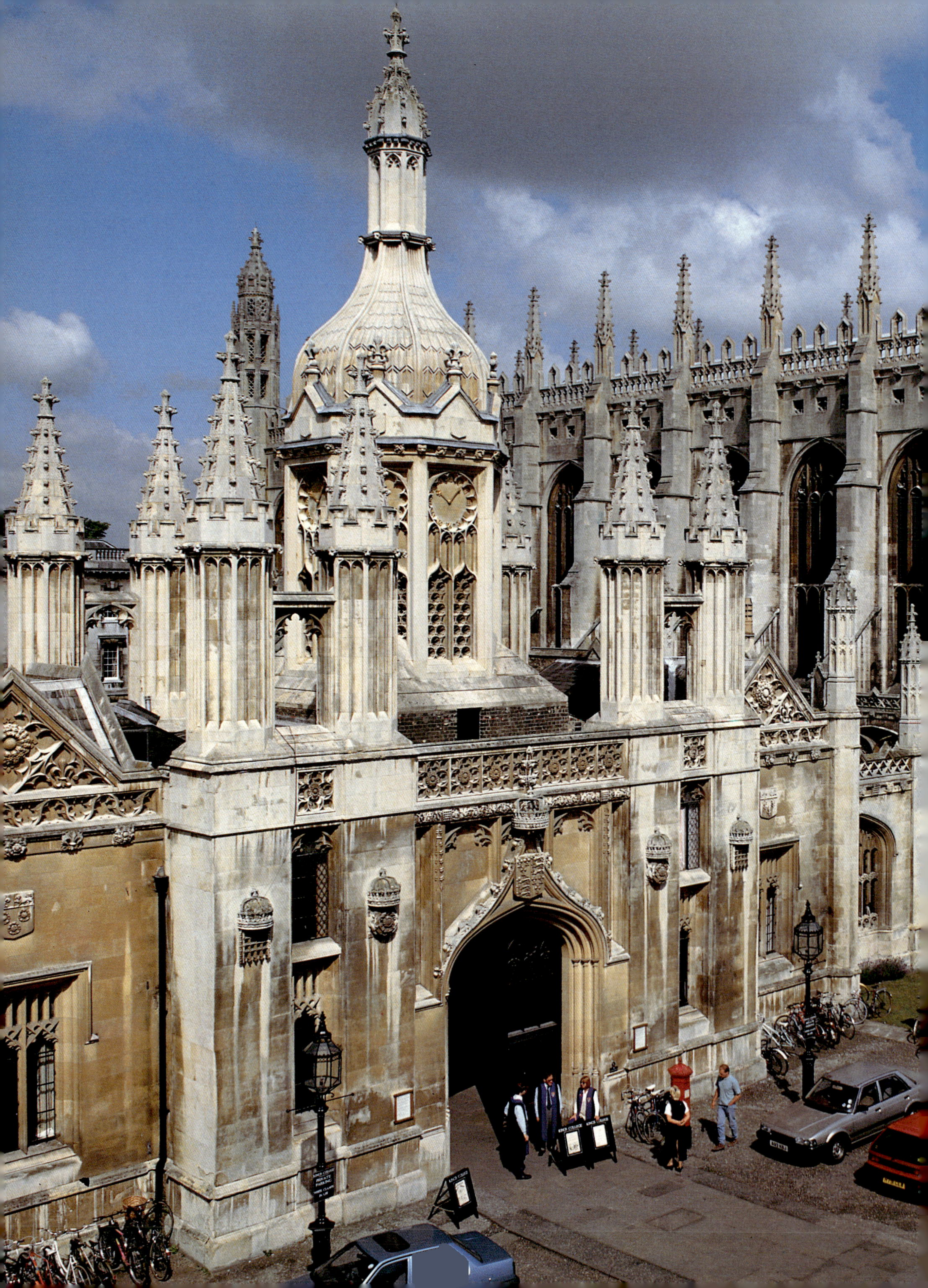

King's College

Le King's (photo pages 16-18) fut fondé sur une échelle audacieuse, digne d'un roi. Plusieurs rues et une église, ainsi qu'au moins un autre collège durent être supprimés pour dégager le site. Mais sa construction dura longtemps.

Contrairement aux habitudes, le collège arbore une architecture simple, sa Great Court ne représentant que trois époques. La construction de la chapelle fut entamée par Henry VI en 1446 et se poursuivit pendant cinq règnes, jusqu'à ce qu'elle fut enfin achevée en 1538 ; seuls des fonds royaux pouvaient la mener à bien.

La voûte à nervures en éventail, les vitraux et les panneaux en bois avec ses blasons de Henry VIII et d'Anne Boleyn, datent du début du XVIe siècle, et sont l'un des sommets de ce style.

Le bâtiment de l'architecte Gibbs date de 1723 dont il a reçu le nom. Il abrite les Fellows et, au XVIIIe siècle, il fut le résultat des plans établis par Hawksmoor et Wren, Gibbs, Adam et Wyatt, pour compléter le collège, mais qui furent abandonnés par manque de fonds.

Queens' College

Le collège (photo ci-dessus) est situé dans Queens' Lane qui rejoignait Trinity Lane jusqu'à la construction de King's. Il tient son nom de Marguerite d'Anjou, épouse d'Henry VI, qui l'établit en 1448, puis d'Elizabeth Woodville, épouse d'Edouard IV, qui le dota.

La Front Court est la première cour en brique de l'université. Elle est restée suffisamment intacte pour donner une très bonne idée de son aspect original. On pense que le cadran peint (photo ci-dessous) date du milieu du XVIIe siècle ; il comporte des soleils et des lunes, ainsi que les signes du zodiaque.

La légende qui veut que le pont de bois (photo page 20) qui enjambe la Cam ait été conçu par un mathématicien du XVIIe siècle, et construit sans fixations, n'est que cela : une légende. Il date de 1749 et fut l'oeuvre d'un maître charpentier ingénieux, nommé Etheridge. Il fut rénové en 1902. Louez une autre barque à fond plat dans le Mill Pool, juste au-dessous du pont.

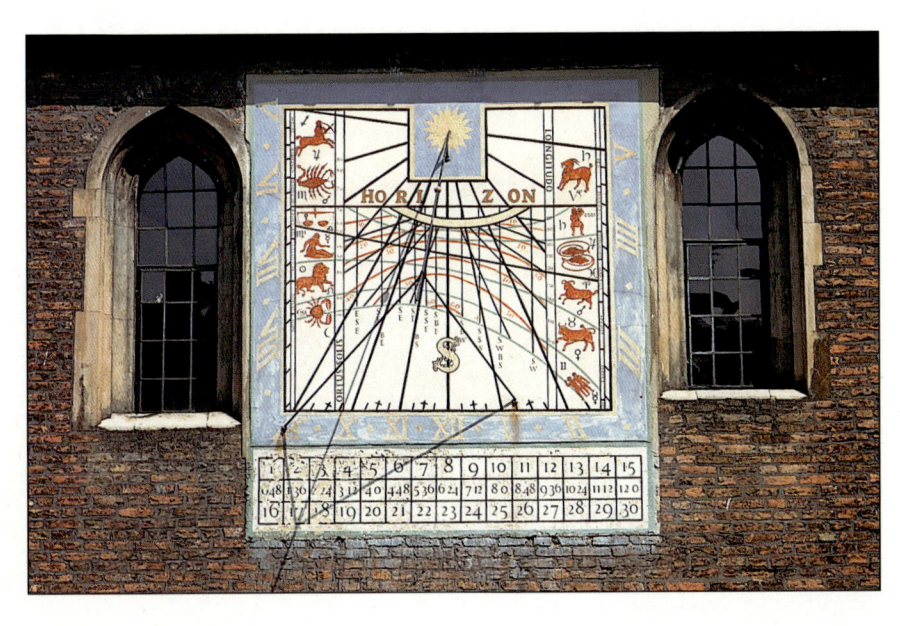

St Catherine's

Cat's fut fondé en 1475 par Robert Woodlark, Principal de King's. L'un des devoirs de ses Fellows était de prier pour le repos de l'âme de ses bienfaiteurs. Il fut complètement reconstruit, puis agrandi au XVIIe et au XVIIIe siècle. Jusqu'au XVIIIe, on entrait au Cat's par l'arrière, en passant par la loge dans Queens' Lane, mais après l'achat et la démolition de maisons, on ouvrit la façade avec ses clôtures.

King's College

King's (Foto Seite 16-18) wurde in großartigem, einem König ziemendem Stil gegründet. Mehrere Straßen mußten dem College Platz machen und eine Kirche und mindestens ein anderes College von seinem Grundstück geräumt werden. Sein Bau dauerte jedoch sehr lange.

Das College ist architektonisch ungewöhnlich schlicht, die Gebäude des Great Court stammen aus nur drei Perioden. Die Chapel(Foto Seite 17) wurde 1446 von Heinrich VI. begonen und durch fünf Herrschaftsperioden hindurch fortgesetzt, bis sie 1538 fertiggestellt war. Nur königliche Finanzen konnten dies erreichen.

Das Fächergewölbe, die Buntglasfenster und der Holzlettner mit seinen Wappenbildern von Heinrich VIII. und Anne Boleyn stammen aus dem frühen 16. Jahrhundert und sind in ihrer Art unübertroffen.

Das Gibbs Building stammt aus dem Jahr 1723 und ist nach seinem Architekten benannt. Hier wohnen die Fellows. Dieses Gebäude war im 18. Jahrhundert das einzige Ergebnis von Plänen für die Fertigstellung des Colleges, die von Hawksmoor und Wren, Gibbs, Adam und Wyatt entworfen, dann aber aus Geldmangel nicht realisiert wurden.

Queens' College

Das College (Foto Seite 19) liegt in der Queens Lane, die bis zum Bau von Kings in die Trinity Lane einmündete. Es erhielt seinen Namen von Königin Margaret von Anjou, der Gemahlin Heinrichs VI., die das College 1448 gründete, und Königin Elizabeth Woodville, der Gemahlin Eduard IV., die es zu einer Stiftung machte.

Front Court ist das erste Court-Gebäude der Universität aus Ziegelstein. Sein heutiges Aussehen vermittelt dem Betrachter einen guten Eindruck dessen, wie es ursprünglich aussah. Die aufgemahlte Sonnenuhr(Foto Seite 19) ist wahrscheinlich aus der Mitte des 17. Jahrhunderts. Sie enthält auch einen Mondkalender und die Sternzeichen.

Die Legende, daß die Holzbrücke über den Cam im 17. Jahrhundert von einem Mathematiker entworfen und ohne Befestigungsteile gebaut wurde, bleibt weiterhin eine Legende. Die Brücke(Foto oben) stammt aus dem Jahr 1749 und war das Werk eines erfindungsreichen Meisterzimmermanns mit Namen Etheridge. Sie wurde 1902 erneuert. Mieten Sie sich im Mill Pool unterhalb der Brücke wieder einen Stechkahn.

St Catherine's

Cat's wurde 1475 von Robert Woodlark, dem Dekan von King's, gegründet. Eine der Pflichten seiner Fellows war es, für die Seelen ihrer Gönner zu beten. St Catherine's wurde im 17. und 18. Jahrhundert neu aufgebaut und vergrößert. Bis zum 18. Jahrhundert lag sein Eingang an der Rückseite, durch das auf die Queens' Lane führende Tor. Durch den Kauf und das Abreißen anderer Häuser konnte die College-Front mit ihren Geländern dann aber geöffnet werden.

Corpus Christi College

Corpus(photo right) was founded by members of the two Cambridge Guilds of Corpus Christi and the Blessed Virgin Mary in 1352. Old Court is tucked away behind St Bene't's Church, with which the Guild of Corpus Christi was linked; initially the undergraduates worshipped in the church, but in about 1500 added a chapel onto it for their own use, linked to Corpus by a gallery over a gateway. Old Court is the earliest fairly complete court at Cambridge and gives the best idea of a 14th-century college, a single court built on an irregular plan with a gateway, hall, buttery and kitchen, master's lodge and chambers. Corpus was more than doubled in size in 1823 when New Court facing onto King's

Parade was built. It was designed by Wilkins and he is here more recognisably the architect of the screen fronting King's than of Downing College or the National Gallery. Corpus has an outstanding collection of pre-Civil War silver, which it held onto it while the other colleges sent theirs to be melted down in aid of King or Parliament.

St Bene't's Church
St Bene't's is Saxon, dating from about 1025, and is the only one of several early churches at Cambridge to survive. It is also the oldest building in the county. In the 13th century, the early University held its assemblies here. The tower is unusually fine, with two carved stone lions on the arch inside, but the rest of the church was largely rebuilt in Victorian times. Campanology, the art of change-ringing, was probably invented here by Fabian Steadman in the 1630s. He will have swung four of the existing bells.

Diagonally opposite Corpus is:

The University Press
This is surely the most smartly housed of publishers. Established in 1584, it goes back to a royal charter 50 years earlier. The present stone building was designed by Edward Blore in 1831, and its grandeur results from the gift of surplus funds subscribed to erect a statue of William Pitt in London. The gigantic oriel window was intended to light a 'handsome room' for the Press's Syndics.

Pembroke College
Stretched along the length of Pembroke Street, the college(photo below) is entered from Trumpington Street. It is named after a countess who founded it on Christmas Eve 1347, and the college porters claim that her confessor haunts it by walking across the top of the Chapel.

The Chapel is a very early work by Wren, built when he was 31 and then more a scientist than an architect. It was given by his uncle Matthew, Bishop of Ely, and the pediment and cupola face onto Trumpington Street.

Little St Mary's
The church is down the lane named after it and behind evergreen trees. It dates from the 1340's and has window tracery as good as that in the Lady Chapel at Ely. Until the 17th century it was both a parish church and the chapel to Peterhouse, to which the chancel is still connected by a 14th century gallery.

Within is a memorial to Godfrey Washington, minister of the church and Fellow of Peterhouse, who died in 1729. His arms are correctly described as argent, 2 bars sable and in chief 3 mullets: 2 stripes and three stars. Are they the origin of the American flag?

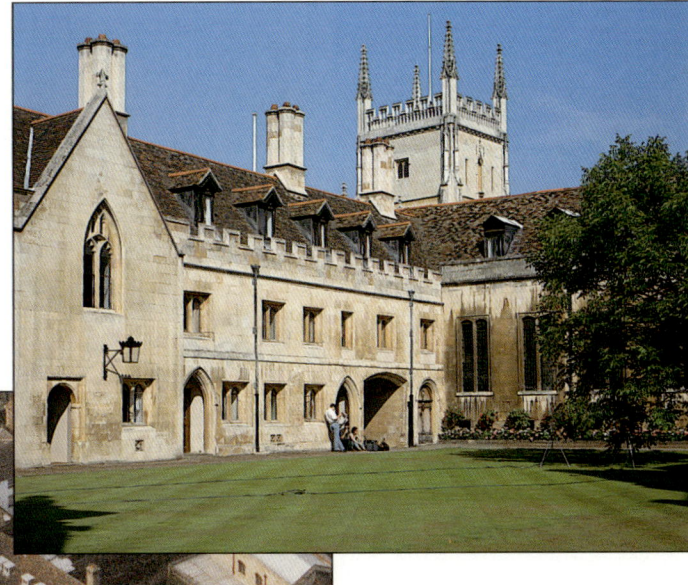

Corpus Christi College
Corpus(photo à gauche) fut fondé en 1352 par les membres de deux confréries religieuses de Cambridge : le Corpus Christi et la Blessed Virgin Mary. Old Court se dissimule derrière l'église St Bene't's, avec laquelle était liée la confrérie du Corpus Christi ; à l'origine, les étudiants se rendaient dans cette église, mais vers 1500, ils ajoutèrent une chapelle réservée à leur propre usage, et reliée à Corpus par une passerelle au-dessus d'une loge.

Old Court qui est la cour pratiquement complète la plus ancienne de Cambridge, donne un aperçu de ce que pouvait être un collège au XIVe siècle. C'est une

Botolph Lane

cour unique construite selon un plan irrégulier avec une loge, un hall, les offices et les cuisines, les corps de logis et les salles du conseil.

En 1823, Corpus occupait plus du double de sa superficie, lorsque fut construite la nouvelle cour qui fait face au King's Parade.

St Bene't's Church

St Bene't est une église saxonne datant de 1025 environ. C'est la seule parmi plusieurs des premières églises de cette époque à subsister à Cambridge. C'est aussi le bâtiment le plus ancien du comté. Au XIIIe siècle, l'université de la première époque y tenait ses assemblées. La tour est particulièrement belle avec ses deux lions sculptés sur l'arcade intérieure, mais le reste de l'église a essentiellement été reconstruit à l'époque victorienne.

En diagonale, en face de Corpus :

The University Press

C'est sans aucun doute la maison d'édition la mieux logée. Etablie en 1584, elle remonte à une charte royale accordée 50 ans auparavant. Le bâtiment actuel en pierre fut conçu par Edward Blore en 1831.

Pembroke College

L'accès au collège qui s'étale sur toute la longueur de Pembroke Street, se fait par Trumpington Street. Il reçut son nom d'une comtesse qui l'institua la veille de Noël 1347, et les concierges du collège affirment que son confesseur vient le hanter en traversant le haut de la chapelle.

La chapelle fut l'une des premières oeuvres édifiées par Wren, qui la construisit alors qu'il n'avait que 31 ans, et était plutôt un scientifique qu'un architecte. (photo page 21)

Little St Mary's

L'église est située au bout de la rue qui porte son nom, derrière un bosquet d'arbres toujours verts. Elle date de vers 1340.

Elle abrite une plaque commémorative de Godfrey Washington, pasteur de l'église et Fellow de Peterhouse, qui mourut en 1729.

Corpus Christi College

Corpus (Foto Seite 21) wurde von Mitgliedern der zwei Cambridge-Gilden Guild of Corpus Christi und Guild of the Blessed Virgin Mary im Jahr 1352 gegründet. Old Court liegt hinter der St Bene't's Church versteckt, mit der die Guild of Corpus Christi verbunden war. Die Studenten besuchten anfänglich die Kirche, etwa um 1500 erhielt das College dann aber eine Kapelle, die über eine Galerie über einem Tor mit Corpus verbunden ist, für seinen Gebrauch.

Old Court ist das früheste ziemlich vollständige Court-Gebäude in Cambridge und vermittelt das Aussehen eines Colleges aus dem 14. Jahrhundert am besten: Ein einziger, auf unregelmäßigem Plan erbauter Court mit einem Torbogen, Halle, Vorratsraum und Küche, Rektorwohnung und Schlafräumen.

Corpus wurde 1823 durch den Bau des auf die Kings's Parade hinausgehenden New Courts größenmäßig mehr als verdoppelt.

22

St Bene't's Church

St Bene't's ist angelsächsisch. Sie stammt etwa aus dem Jahr 1025 und ist die einzige mehrerer früher Kirchen in Cambridge, die heute noch steht. Sie ist gleichzeitig das älteste Gebäude in der Grafschaft. Im 13. Jahrhundert hielt die frühe Universität ihre Morgenandachten hier ab. Der Turm ist ungewöhnlich schön und hat innen einen Bogen mit zwei Steinlöwen. Der Rest der Kirche wurde jedoch in der viktorianischen Zeit weitgehend umgebaut.

Schräg gegenüber von Corpus liegt die

University Press

Dies ist sicherlich der Verlag mit dem vornehmsten Gebäude. Er wurde 1584 gegründet und geht auf einen 50 Jahre zuvor gewährten königlichen Freibrief zurück. Das heutige Steingebäude wurde 1831 von Edward Blore entworfen.

Pembroke College

Das College (Foto Seite 21) erstreckt sich entlang der Pembroke Street, sein Eingang liegt in der Trumpington Street. Es wurde nach einer Gräfin benannt, die es am Heiligabend 1347 gründete. Die Collegepförtner behaupten, daß der Geist ihres Beichtvaters auf dem Dach der Kapelle umgeht.

Die Kapelle ist ein sehr frühes Werk des Architekten Wren. Sie wurde gebaut, als er 31 Jahre alt und noch mehr ein Wissenschaftler als ein Architekt war.

Little St Mary's

Die Kirche befindet sich hinter immergrünen Bäumen in der nach ihr benannten Straße. Sie stammt aus den 40er Jahren des 13. Jahrhunderts.
In ihr befindet sich ein Denkmal an Godfrey Washington, Pastor der Kirche und Fellow von Peterhouse, der 1729 starb.

Peterhouse

Here is the oldest college,(photo below) founded in 1280. The original hall and buttery are the earliest college buildings at Cambridge. They are on the left of Old Court, which is mostly mediaeval although refaced. The passage at the far end is so drafty that the student Frank Whittle is supposed to have had the idea for the jet engine here.

Matthew Wren donated the Chapel, the first of two such gifts to colleges, while Master in 1625-35. It very curiously interweaves Gothic and Classical designs. The college buildings are attractively varied, and one of the best views of them must belong to the Master, whose Lodge is the fine Queen Anne house opposite.

The Fitzwilliam Museum

The University had no proper museum until the 7th Viscount Fitzwilliam bequeathed it his collections, library, and money to house them in 1816. The building(photo page 24) was begun in 1837 and has a generous feel to it, with a rich and splendid interior. It houses collections of antiquities and the fine and applied arts which are possibly the best outside London.

Hobson's Conduit

The 'Conduit' or fountain(photo page 24) stands at the corner of Benet Place and dates from 1614. Until 1856 it stood in the Market Place, but it still functions and is the visible feature of the Conduit. This is an early water supply for cleaning the streets and the King's Ditch, a mediaeval defence which had degenerated by 1610 into an odorous drain. The whole utility was given to Cambridge by Thomas Hobson, who ran a business hiring out horses. "Hobson's Choice" refers to his practice of allowing customers to 'choose' their horses only on a first-in, first-out basis.

Peterhouse

C'est le plus ancien collège, (photo page 23) qui fut fondé en 1280. Le hall et les offices originaux constituent les bâtiments collégiaux les plus anciens de Cambridge. Ils sont situés sur la gauche de l'Old Court, dont l'aspect est principalement médiéval, bien qu'elle ait subi des ravalements.

Matthew Wren a fait don de la chapelle, la première de deux donations de ce genre aux collèges, alors qu'il était Principal en 1625-35. Elle intègre curieusement le style gothique et le style classique. Les bâtiments du collège présentent une variété élégante et l'un des meilleurs points de vue en est réservé au Principal, dont la loge est la magnifique maison de style Queen Anne, située en face.

Le Fitzwilliam Museum

L'université n'avait pas de musée lui appartenant en propre jusqu'à ce qu'en 1816, le 7ème vicomte Fitzwilliam lui lègue ses collections, sa bibliothèque et de l'argent pour les abriter.(photo à droite)

Il regroupe des collections d'objets d'antiquités, ainsi que des oeuvres d'art et des objets d'artisanat qui sont probablement les plus belles en dehors de Londres.

Hobson's Conduit

Le "Conduit", une fontaine, (photo ci-dessous) qui se tient au coin de Benet Place, date de 1614. Jusqu'en 1856, elle se dressait sur la place du marché, mais elle fonctionne toujours et constitue la partie visible du Conduit.

Peterhouse

Hier befindet sich das älteste College, (Foto Seite 23) das 1280 gegründet wurde. Die ursprüngliche Halle und der Vorratsraum sind die ältesten Collegegebäude in Cambridge. Sie liegen links vom Old Court, der hauptsächlich mittelalterlich ist, jedoch eine neuere Fassade hat.

Matthew Wren stiftete die Kapelle, das erste von zwei derartigen Geschenken an Colleges, während er 1625 bis 1635 Rektor war. Sie umfaßt eine seltsame Verschmelzung gothischer und klassischer Entwürfe. Die College-Gebäude sind attraktiv unterschiedlich. Wohl den besten Blick auf sie hat der Rektor, dessen Wohnung das gegenüberliegende prächtige Haus im Queen-Anne-Stil ist.

Das Fitzwilliam Museum

Die Universität hatte kein richtiges Museum, bis der 7. Viscount Fitzwilliam ihm 1816 seine Sammlungen, Bibliothek und Geld für ihre Unterbringung vermachte. Es enthält Sammlungen von Antiquitäten und der schönen und angewandten Künste, die möglicherweise die besten außerhalb Londons sind.(Foto oben)

Hobson's Conduit

Der "Conduit"(Foto unten,links) ist ein aus dem Jahr 1614 stammender Brunnen an der Ecke von Benet Place. Bis 1856 stand er auf dem Marktplatz. Er funktioniert immer noch und ist das sichtbare Merkmal des "Conduit".

Below: One of the exhibits on exploration of the arctic & antarctic which can be seen at the Scott Polar Reasearch Institute in Lensfield Road.

L'un des objets utilisés lors de l'exploration de l'Arctique et de l'Antarctique, que l'on peut admirer à l'Institut Scott sur la recherche polaire dans Lensfield Road

Eines der Ausstellungsstüke über die Erforschung von Arktik und Antarktik im Scott Polar Research Institute in Lensfield Road.

Around And About Cambridge

Cambridge is at the centre of fairly flat country. Until the draining programme of the 17th century the area to the north was so wet that it was called the Isle of Ely and effectively the King left it to the Bishop to administer. It is still an area of rivers and dykes and agriculture, with small country towns and villages, largely untroubled by the industrialism of modern life.

Ely Cathedral

Approaching from Cambridge, across land that was once waterlogged, the first sight is of towers and leads, shimmering on a hot day. Ely is a charming place to walk about and still has a mediaeval sense of scale in which the Cathedral dominates.

The Cathedral(photo below) is Norman but much of its architectural distinction dates from the 14th century. The Octagon, the great central tower, was built in 1322 when a Norman one collapsed and the opportunity was seized to build something spectacular in its place. Like the Lady Chapel of the same period, it is best seen from within, and is a triumph of mediaeval engineering. At the east end is the splendid chantry chapel of Bishop Alcock, founder of Jesus College, Cambridge, with more cockerel rebuses. Several bishops of Ely took a great interest in the University. To the south you may stroll through the extensive remains of the Benedictine monastery. Henry VIII abolished it in 1539 and founded the King's School instead, so boys now study where once the monks lived. The priory entrance was through the great 14th-century gatehouse called the Porta, facing onto The Gallery

Oliver Cromwell's House, Ely

Cromwell lived at what is now 29, St Mary's Street in 1636-46. The house,(photo page 26) like many in Ely, was already old in his time and contains a 16th-century wall-painting. After having various uses, such as the Cromwell Arms and as a vicarage, it is now the Tourist Information Office and a centre for guided tours of the Cathedral and town. Part of it is open to visitors, furnished as in Cromwell's day.

Dans Les Environs De Cambridge

Cambridge est située au centre d'une campagne assez plane. Jusqu'aux travaux d'assainissement entrepris au XVIIe siècle, la région au nord était si humide qu'on la désignait sous le nom d'île d'Ely, et en fait, le roi en laissait l'administration à l'évêque. C'est encore une région de rivières et de digues, consacrée à l'agriculture, avec de petits villages et bourgades, qui ont essentiellement été épargnés par l'industrialisation de la vie moderne.

Ely Cathedral

En venant de Cambridge, à travers une campagne qui était jadis recouverte de marécages, on entr'aperçoit ses tours et ses toitures de plomb, miroitant par les jours de grande chaleur. Ely est un endroit charmant pour s'y promener. Elle a conservé ses proportions médiévales, où domine la cathédrale.

La cathédrale (photo page 25) romane est un monument dont la plus grande partie de l'architecture remonte au XIVe siècle. L'octogone, la grande tour centrale, fut construit en 1322 après l'effondrement de la tour romane, ce qui donna l'occasion de construire à sa place un bâtiment spectaculaire. Comme la Lady Chapel de la même époque, elle vaut vraiment un coup d'oeil à l'intérieur, car c'est un triomphe d'architecture médiévale.

Maison D'Oliver Cromwell, Ely

Cromwell vécut de 1636 à 1646 à ce qui est aujourd'hui le 29, St Mary's Street.

Après avoir servi à de multiples fins, telles que le Cromwell Arms et comme maison du pasteur, elle abrite désormais l'office du tourisme, et sert de centre aux visites guidées dans la cathédrale et dans la ville. Une partie en est ouverte aux visiteurs, où le mobilier est le même qu'à l'époque de Cromwell.(photo ci-dessus)

Cambridge - Seine Umgebung

Cambridge liegt in der Mitte einer ziemlich flachen Gegend. Das Gebiet nördlich der Stadt war bis zu einem Trockenlegungsprogramm im 17. Jahrhundert so naß, daß es die "Isle of Ely" genannt wurde und der König seine Verwaltung effektiv dem Bischof überließ. Auch heute noch ist es eine Gegend mit vielen Flüssen und Dämmen, viel Landwirtschaft und kleinen ländlichen Städten und Dörfern, die vom Industrialismus der heutigen Zeit weitgehend ungestört bleiben.

Ely Cathedral

Bei der Anreise von Cambridge her über einen früher einmal sumpfigen Landstrich sieht man als erstes Türme und Bleidächer, die an heißen Tagen in der Sonne glänzen. Ely ist ein bezaubernder Ort, der zur Erkundung zu Fuß einlädt. Sein Größenmaßstab mit der die Stadt dominierenden Kathedrale mutet noch immer mittelalterlich an.

Die Kathedrale (Foto Seite 25) ist normannisch, ihr architektonischer Rang geht jedoch weitgehend auf das 14. Jahrhundert zurück. Das Octagon, der große mittlere Turm, wurde 1322 gebaut, als ein normannischer Turm einstürzte und man die Gelegenheit ergriff, um an seiner Stelle ein spektakuläres Bauwerk zu errichten. Wie die Lady Chapel aus der gleichen Zeit zeigt auch sie sich im Inneren von ihrer besten Seite. Sie ist ein Triumph mittelalterlicher Bautechnik.

Oliver Cromwell's House, Ely

1636 bis 1646 wohnte Cromwell in diesem Haus (Foto oben) mit der heutigen Anschrift 29, St Mary's Street. Es wurde auf verschiedene Arten genutzt, wie z.B. als Gasthaus mit dem Namen Cromwell Arms und als Pfarrhaus, und ist heute das Touristeninformationsbüro und ein Zentrum für Führungen durch die Kathedrale und die Stadt. Ein Teil des Hauses ist wie in Cromwells Zeit eingerichtet und steht Besuchern offen.

Ely Cathedral

Wicken Fen

The 605 acres of Wicken are the remains of the Great Fen, drained almost to extinction. It is a place of waterlogging, of sedges, reeds, herbs and hayfields, of dragonflies, marsh peas and bladderwort, bog myrtle and guelder roses. There are longer and shorter walks (one on boards), a tower hide and good visitors' centre.

Newmarket

Newmarket means horse-racing, and where better to start than at the National Horseracing Museum? It is housed in the old Subscription Rooms (99 High Street), a place where jockeys, punters and trainers used to meet. Works of art and all manner of exhibits associated with the sport are attractively displayed here, and there is much to interest the layman. Guided tours of the racing attractions start here. Visit the gallops, studs and training yards and see famous horses.

Wicken Fen

Les 245 hectares de Wicken constituent les restes de la région des Great Fens, pratiquement asséché jusqu'à extinction.

C'est une région de marécages, joncs, roseaux, fines herbes et champs de foin, libellules, pois gris des marais, utriculaires, myrtes des marais et boules de neige de Gueldre où le National Trust continue d'appliquer les méthodes de gestion traditionnelles.

Newmarket

Newmarket est synonyme de courses de chevaux, et où pourrait-on mieux commencer que par le National Horseracing Museum ? Ce musée des courses de chevaux est logé dans les anciennes Subscription Rooms, au no. 99 High Street, un endroit où se rencontraient les jockeys, les parieurs et les entraîneurs. Des objets d'art et toutes sortes d'objets intéressants liés à ce sport y sont exposés de manière attrayante, et il y a beaucoup de choses qui intéresseront le néophyte.
Les visites guidées des hauts-lieux des courses commencent ici. Visitez les pistes de galop, les haras et les paddocks d'entraînement, et venez voir des chevaux célèbres.

Newmarket

Wicken Fen

Die 5025 a von Wicken sind die Reste der Great Fen genannten Moorlandschaft, die fast bis zur völligen Zerstörung trockengelegt wurde.

Wicken Fen ist ein sumpfiges Gebiet mit Riedgräsern, Schilf, Kräutern und Heufeldern, mit Libellen und seltenen Sumpfpflanzen. Der National Trust bewirtschaftet das Gebiet mit traditionellen Methoden.

Newmarket

Newmarket bedeutet Pferderennen - der beste Ausgangspunkt für einen Besuch dieser Stadt ist wohl das National Horseracing Museum. Es befindet sich in den alten Subscription Rooms (99 High Street), wo sich früher Jockeys, Spieler und Trainer trafen. Kunstwerke und alle Arten verschiedener, mit dem Sport verbundener Artikel sind hier ausgestellt und bieten auch dem Laien viel Interessantes.

Führungen der Rennsport-Attraktionen beginnen hier. Besuchen Sie die "Gallops", Gestüte und Trainingshöfe und sehen Sie berühmte Pferde.

The Imperial War Museum At Duxford

Duxford(photo below) is an historic fighter station, operational from March 1918. In the Second World War it was associated first with Douglas Bader and then with the US 8th Air Force, who had 200,000 men here. It claims to be the biggest and best aeroplane museum in Europe. The collection is truly international and as well as military craft, there are civil planes,(including Concord) fighting vehicles, unmanned reconnaisance drones, torpedoes and half a British submarine, scuttled during an attempt on the Turpitz. It is also a working museum, with frequent event-days.

Wimpole Hall

This large house has for long been owned by collectors and has several times been a great treasure-house. This is reflected in the fine quality of the interior. The house is mainly 18th-century and the principal architect James Gibbs, with interesting alterations, early works by John Soane. The park was enlarged and improved by Capability Brown in 1769 and views of it were painted on Catherine the Great's famous Russian dinner service. The house is now a National Trust property.

Wimpole Home Farm

It was the 3rd Earl of Hardwicke, President of the Board of Agriculture in 1804, who built the New Model Farm. Soane's farm buildings of 1794 have been restored to house a history of farming, with a large display of farm implements. All around is an officially recognised centre for rare breeds of farm animal and poultry.

The American Military Cemetery At Madingley

This is a place of peace, beautifully kept in tribute to the dead.(photos above)

Yet it has a positive feel, the long Wall of the Missing contrasting with views through a landscape fringed with mature trees towards Cambridge, less than two miles away. The Memorial Chapel, the work of American architects and craftsmen, uses English materials in an un-English way to detail American involvement in the Second World War.

Imperial War Museum A Duxford

Duxford(photo ci-dessous) est une station de combat historique, en activité depuis mars 1918. Pendant la deuxième Guerre Mondiale, son nom fut associé tout d'abord avec Douglas Bader, puis avec la 8ème Force de l'Air américaine qui y comptait 200.000 hommes. Elle revendique le musée d'aéronefs le plus vaste et le plus complet d'Europe.

Wimpole Hall

Cette imposante demeure appartient de longue date à des collectionneurs et a contenu à plusieurs reprises des trésors, ce qui se retrouve dans la qualité superbe de son décor intérieur, cadre digne de la vie du connaisseur.

Cette demeure date principalement du XVIIIe siècle dont l'architecte principal fut James Gibb, des modifications intéressantes ayant été l'oeuvre au début de la carrière de John Soane.

Wimpole Home Farm

Il s'agit d'un centre officiellement agréé pour l'élevage de races rares d'animaux de la ferme et de volailles.

Cimetière Militaire Americain De Madingley

Cet endroit paisible est méticuleusement entretenu en hommage aux morts.(photo page 28)

Il en émane pourtant une impression positive, le long Mur des Absents contrastant avec le panorama qui se dégage à travers un paysage bordé de grands arbres en direction de Cambridge, à moins de cinq kilomètres de là.

Das Imperial War Museum In Duxford

Duxford (Foto Seite 28) ist eine historische Jagdflugzeugstation, die ab März 1918 in Betrieb war. Im 2. Weltkrieg war es zuerst mit Douglas Bader und dann mit der 8. US Air Force assoziiert, die 200.000 Mann hier stationierte. Duxford verfügt über das größte und beste Flugzeugmuseum in Europa.

Wimpole Hall

Dieses große Haus war lange Zeit im Besitz von Sammlern und war schon mehrmals ein großes Schatzhaus. Dies spiegelt sich in der vorzüglichen Qualität seines Interieurs wieder, das die Kulisse für das Leben des Kunstgenießers ist.

Das Haus ist weitgehend im Stil des 18. Jahrhunderts erbaut. Der Hauptarchitekt war James Gibbs. Es umfaßt einige interessante Änderungen, frühe Werke von John Soane.

Wimpole Home Farm

Wimpole Home Farm ist ein offiziell anerkanntes Zentrum für seltene Nutztier- und Geflügelrassen.

Der amerikanische Militärfriedoff in Madingley

Ein friedvolles, vorzüglich instandgehaltenes Denkmal an die Gefallenen. Trotzdem verleiht es ein positives Gefühl. Die lange Mauer mit den Namen der Vermißten hebt sich ab vom Ausblick durch eine von großen Bäumen eingefaßte Landschaft in Richtung Cambridge (das knapp 3 km entfernt ist). (Foto Seite 28)

Houghton Mill

Houghton is an attractive village with many pretty half-timbered cottages and a thatched market cross. Through it flows the Ouse, with its willows and swans and a large weather-boarded and brick mill. Picturesquely sited, it has hoists projecting from the roofs. The mill(photo left) is occasionally open to the public. It is a National Trust property.

St Ives

A relatively unspoilt market town (photos page 30) also on the Ouse, it has several pleasant streets of Stuart and Georgian houses and shops, in the local red and later yellow brick. Bridge Street has few modern intrusions, but ancient alleys and courtyards. It leads to the bridge dating from 1415, with its Chapel of St Lawrence, one of only two bridge chapels outside Yorkshire. In the cobbled Market Hill is a Victorian statue of Oliver Cromwell, who lived here in 1631-36.

Peterborough Cathedral

Like Ely, Peterborough Cathedral(photo page 31) was Norman with a Benedictine monastery serving it.
Although begun in 1118, it was not finished until 1238 which is why the magnificent west front is gothic. The 'New Building' at the east end has fan-vaulting which may be where John Wastell perfected his idea for the great vaults of King's College. The ceilings of the nave c.1220 is of painted wood, the model for

Victorian ones at Ely. The transepts ceilings, also of wood, no longer have their original painted patterns. The brass eagle lectern has remained in use since monastic times and has an inscription that it was the gift of Abbot William de Ramsey (1471-96) and John Malden, Prior. The most attractive part of the city is the Cathedral precinct. In 1541 the monastic buildings, mainly on the south side, were converted into canons' houses and the abbot's house became the Bishop's Palace. Just within Outer Gate on the right is the King's Lodging and the Abbot's Prison.

Houghton Mill

Houghton est un charmant village aux nombreux jolis cottages à colombage, qui possède une croix de marché recouverte d'un toit de chaume. Il est traversé par l'Ouse, avec ses saules pleureurs et ses cygnes, ainsi qu'un grand moulin (photo page 29) en brique aux planches à recouvrement.

St Ives

Plusieurs rues agréables de cette bourgade relativement bien conservée, dans la vallée de l'Ouse, possèdent des maisons et boutiques de l'époque des rois Stuart et du roi George, en briques locales rouges, puis plus tard jaunes. Bridge Street a quelques rares intrusions modernes, mais aussi des allées et des cours anciennes.(photo page 30)

Peterborough Cathedral

Tout comme Ely, Peterborough Cathedral(photo ci-dessous) était romane avec un monastère la desservant. Bien que commencée en 1118, elle ne fut achevée qu'en 1238 ce qui explique que la façade ouest soit gothique. Le "nouveau bâtiment", du côté est, a une voûte en éventail et c'est peut-être là que John Wastell perfectionna sa conception pour les grandes voûtes du King's College. Les plafonds de la nef et les transepts sont en bois peint ; ils ont servi de modèle pour les plafonds de l'époque victorienne de la cathédrale d'Ely.

Houghton Mill

Houghton ist ein attraktives Dorf mit vielen hübschen Häusern mit Fachwerk und reedgedecktem Marktkreuz. Durch das Dorf fließt die von Weiden gesäumte Ouse mit ihren Schwänen und einem großen verschalten und gemauerten Mühlhaus. (Foto Seite 29)

St Ives

Ein ebenfalls an der Ouse liegender, relativ unberührter Marktflecken mit mehreren anmutigen Straßen mit aus örtlichem rotem und später gelben Ziegelstein gebauten Häusern und Läden im Stuart- und georgianischen Stil. In Bridge Street finden sich einige moderne Gebäude, aber auch alte Gassen und Höfe. (Foto Seite 30)

Peterborough Cathedral

Wie Ely Cathedral ist auch Peterborough Cathedral (Foto unten) normannisch. Sie war ebenfalls an ein Kloster angeschlossen. Mit ihrem Bau wurde schon 1118 begonnen, sie wurde aber erst im Jahr 1238 fertiggestellt. Dies ist der Grund dafür, warum die prachtvolle Westfront gothisch ist. Das "New Building" (neue Gebäude) am Ostende der Kathedrale hat ein Fächergewölbe. Es kann sein, daß John Wastell seine Idee für die großartigen Gewölbe von King´s College hier zur Perfektion ausreifen ließ. Die Decken in Hauptschiff und Querschiffen sind aus bemaltem Holz und bilden das Modell für die viktorianischen Decken in der Ely Cathedral.

A1309/A10 ELY
FITZWILLIAM COLLEGE
HUNTINGDON ROAD
A604
HUNTINGDON, ST IVES,
PETERBOROUGH & HAUGHTON MILL
CASTLE PARK
CARLYLE ROAD
ALPHA ROAD
HERTFORD STREET
CASTLE STREET
NEW HALL
ST EDMUND'S
HOUSE
SHELLEY ROW
CASTLE ROW
CASTLE MOUND
CHESTERTON ROAD
SWIMMING
POOL
VICTORIA AVENUE
MOUNT PLEASANT
ST PETER'S ST
CHESTERTON LANE
JESUS GREEN
LUCY CAVENDISH
COLLEGE
HAYMARKET RD
KETTLES YARD
MAGDALENE
COLLEGE
PARK PARADE
MADINGLEY ROAD
LADY MARGARET RD
POUND HILL
A45
AMERICAN MILITARY
CEMETERY
WESTMINSTER
(THEOLOGICAL)
NORTHAMPTON STREET
MAGDALENE STREET
NEW PARK ST
PUNTS
QUAYSIDE
THOMPSON'S LANE
JESUS COLLEGE
MIDSUMMER
SCHOOL OF
PYTHAGORAS
PORTUGAL PLACE
ST JOHN'S COLLEGE
ROUND CHURCH ST
PARK ST
WESLEY
HOUSE
BRUNSWICK WALK
HOLY SEPULCHRE
(ROUND CHURCH)
ADC
THEATRE
MALCOLM STREET
JESUS LANE
MAIDS CAUSEWAY
BRIDGE OF SIGHS
ST JOHN'S ST
BRIDGE ST
SIDNEY SUSSEX
COLLEGE
KING ST
SHORT STREET
GRANGE ROAD
QUEEN'S ROAD
ALL SAINT'S
PASSAGE
SIDNEY ST
SUSSEX ST
CHRIST'S PIECES
TRINITY
COLLEGE
GREEN STREET
TRINITY LANE
TRINITY ST
ROSE CRES
CHRIST'S COLLEGE
PUNTS
GONVILLE & CAIUS
COLLEGE
BUS STATION
EMMANUEL ROAD
ELM STREET
GARRET HOSTEL LANE
TRINITY
HALL
ST MARY'S ST
GREAT
ST MARY'S
CHURCH
SENATE HOUSE
DRUMMER STREET
ORCHARD ST
CLARENDON ST
OLD SCHOOLS
PETTY CURY
ROBINSON COLLEGE
MEMORIAL
COURT
CLARE COLLEGE
KING'S COLLEGE
CHAPEL
ST MARY'S
PASSAGE
LION YARD
GUILDHALL
PARKER STREET
EMMANUEL ST
MELBOURNE PLACE
UNIVERSITY
LIBRARY
THE BACKS
KING'S
COLLEGE
WHEELER ST
KING'S PARADE
BENE'T ST
EMMANUEL
COLLEGE
CORN EXCHANGE ST
HISTORY OF
SCIENCE
ST BENE'T'S
CHURCH
FREE SCHOOL LANE
PARKSIDE
ZOOLOGY
MUSEUM
KING'S LANE
WHIPPLE
MUSEUM
DOWNING STREET
DOWNING PLACE
ST ANDREW'S ST
PARK TERRACE
ST CATHERINE'S
COLLEGE
SEDGWICK
MUSEUM
QUEEN'S LANE
WEST ROAD
CORPUS CHRISTI
COLLEGE
MUSEUM OF
ARCHAEOLOGY
& ANTHROPOLOGY
PARKER'S PIECE
QUEEN'S
COLLEGE
MATHEMATICAL
BRIDGE
PEMBROKE ST
MUSEUM OF
GEOLOGY
PEMBROKE
COLLEGE
REGENT STREET
REGENT TERRACE
SIDGWICK SITE
(UNIVERSITY DEPTS)
MILL POOL
MILL LANE
SILVER STREET
PUNTS
GRANTA PL
LITTLE ST MARY'S LANE
LITTLE
ST MARY'S
CHURCH
TENNIS COURT TER
DOWNING
COLLEGE
GONVILLE
SELWYN COLLEGE
MUSEUM OF CLASSICAL
ARCHAEOLOGY
PETERHOUSE
COLLEGE
FITZWILLIAM ST
SIDGWICK AVENUE
DARWIN COLLEGE
RIDLEY HALL RD
RIDLEY HALL
(THEOLOGICAL)
FITZWILLIAM
MUSEUM
TRUMPINGTON STREET
TENNIS COURT ROAD
NEWNHAM COLLEGE
NEWNHAM WALK
COE FEN
LENSFIELD ROAD
SCOTT POLAR
REAEARCH
INSTITUTE
CHURCH RATE WALK
SHEEPS GREEN
BENET PLACE
SUMMERFIELD
HOBSON'S
CONDUIT
FEN CAUSEWAY
ST ELIGIUS
PLACE
UNION ROAD
NEWNHAM
LANGUAGE
CENTRE
CLARE ROAD
NEWNHAM ROAD
PEMBERTON TER.
PANTON STREET
CORONATION STREET
LAMMAS LAND
ST ELIGIUS STREET
BARTON ROAD
BROOKSIDE
TRUMPINGTON ROAD
A603/B1042
BIGGLESWADE
BEDFORD
COE FEN
BATEMAN STREET
A10 ROYSTON
M11 LONDON
TO THE IMPERIAL WAR
MUSEUM AT DUXFORD
CAMBRIDGE UNIVERSITY
BOTANIC GARDENS